Starry Messengers

By

Alison Chester-Lambert

For Ray,
Hope you enjoy it,
very best wishes
Alison x

In honour of the astrologer Galileo, who looked at the sky through a telescope for the first time in 1609, exactly 400 years ago. He wrote a book of his discoveries that was published in March 1610 and called it `The Starry Messenger`.

ISBN: 978-0-9563677-0-9

Printed by Athenaeum Press Ltd
Gateshead, Tyne and Wear NE11 0PZ

Published by the Midlands School of Astrology
43, St Georges Way
Tamworth
Staffordshire
B77 3HH

01827 68288

e-mail alison@midlandsschoolofastrology.co.uk
web site www.midlandsschoolofastrology.co.uk

DEDICATION

This book is dedicated to my beautiful and talented daughter Jessica, a triple Leo whose personal achievements have already been magnificent.

Acknowledgements

My journey could not have begun without those who taught me astrology. The greatest influences were Linda Goodman, Jonathan Cainer, Clare Martin, Sue Tompkins, Glenn Parry, Liz Greene, Christine Valentine, Richard Idemon and Alexander Von Schlieffen. Special mention goes to Melanie Reinhart who urged me to write this book and get a web site in 2006. I wouldn`t have done either without her encouragement.

My journey into teaching would not have happened without the request of Sue O, manager of the Cottage Healing Centre in Tamworth, who booked me to run my first course. Thanks to Sue and all the students on that first course.

The journey into the Dwarf Planets could not have happened without the team of astronomers that discovered them: Mike Brown, Chad Trujillo and David Rabinowitz. I would like to thank them for the careful and sensitive choice of names, which made it all so easy. Astronomers don`t usually acknowledge astrologers, but Bill Law of the Walsall Astronomy Group has been great at supplying me with loads of interesting stuff and deserves a mention.

And the journey continues because of the support of my current astrology students, who attend my Saturday, Friday and Monday classes. They have faithfully promised me that *one* day they will learn all the glyphs! Thanks to Anne, Anne, Jenny, Maureen, Sue, Maggi, Yoie, Ann, Jayne, Fiona, Gill, Jayne, Andy, Allyson, Betty, Sharon, Karen, Sue, Deb and Lynda. Especially to Maggi who proof read the Haumea chapter after I had lost the will to go on!

Finally, a big thanks to my ex-husband for all the illustrations. This is probably the first and only time that we have managed a joint project without fighting! We leave the results to our beautiful and talented daughter, Jessica, who surpasses both of us with her brilliance and courage.

And finally, thank you to you for buying it! - Alison, March 2009

CONTENTS

Acknowledgements 4

Chapter 1 **CHANGES ARE HAPPENING** 11

"Lo, there is a star in the East…" 11

How can changes to the solar system convey new spiritual meaning? 12

How our knowledge of the solar system has changed 14

The discovery of a whole new region of the Solar System 18

We will discover what our world was created from, why and how 19

Chapter 2 **COOL SCIENCE** 21

Mind-boggling new scientific discoveries.

Why are we making all these discoveries now? 21

What is matter? What is our universe made of? 22

A parallel universe or other dimension that supports ours 23

According to science, you have a dark super-body! 23

What is the God particle? 24

A nine billion dollar experiment called the Large Hadron Collider 25

Most of the matter out in Space is missing too 26

Dark matter in the Universe 27

Dark energy in the Universe 28

The dark part of our own bodies, our soul and spirit,

gets messages from the 96% 28

An explanation simple enough for my mother to understand! 30

Chapter 3 CERES, GODDESS OF GROWING AND GRIEVING
A Great Earth Mother Goddess 33

The dwarf planet 33

The Spiritual Meaning of Ceres 34

The myth of Demeter and Persephone 36

The Eleusinian Mysteries and life after death, a guide into the Underworld 39

Protector of life and death cycle, ensuring re-birth and growth 40

Isis, the Egyptian goddess 41

The ancient mysteries of Egypt 42

The Egyptian Book of the Dead 44

The return of the great goddess after an absence of over 1,000 years 45

Why Ceres Will Be Important in the 21st Century 45

How Ceres will represent food supply after 2006 45

Growing babies. Child abduction and separation. Madeleine McCann 46

Cycles and the passage of time 47

Ceres supports us through death and bereavement 47

Ceres and the parent/child bond. Parent/child issues 49

Some final thoughts 50

Chapter 4 **PLUTO, LORD OF THE INVISIBLE REALMS** 53

So where has Pluto gone to? 53

The Mythology and Ancient Stories of Pluto 54

Pluto as ruler of the Underworld in Roman and Greek Mythology 54

The story of Adam and Eve in the Christian Bible 55

Siva the destroyer and transformer 57

The rise and rise of our fascination with ancient Egypt 59

Egyptian god Ptah "He Who Made All and Created the Gods" 61

The goddess Tiamat from the Sumerian tablets of creation 62

The Sumerian (Iraqi) goddess called Erishkigal 63

The Meaning of Pluto in Astrology 65

The discovery of Pluto the planet 65

The traditional meaning of Pluto in astrology 65

Pluto and the number 9 67

The serpent as a symbol of healing and magic 69

The difference between dark Feminine and dark Masculine 71

What We Can Expect to Gain, Change and Develop in the 21st Century? 72

We shall find parallel universes - the Underworld and Heaven of mythology 72

The changes to Pluto coincide with the development of the Large Hadron Collider 73

The development and acceptance of nuclear energy 76

Can we change our perception of evil and the Devil? 77

Understanding the meaning of life can change our attitude to death and the afterlife 79

Miraculous healing potential, reiki and kundalini 80

Transformation, evolution and `wealth` on a soul level 81

Chapter 5 CHARON, PASSPORT TO PLUTO AND THE INVISIBLE REALMS 83

Charon, a partner for Pluto 83

How Charon was discovered 84

Charon struggling to be accepted 85

The mythological world of ancient Greece and how this might represent the Multiverse 86

The myths of Charon, Nix and Hydra from the Underworld 87

The Spiritual Meaning of Charon 89

The Importance of the ferryman in significant ancient texts 89

A symbol of the beginning of an immense and epic journey of discovery for the human race 89

What does duality mean? 90

Chapter 6 **MAKEMAKE, GREAT SEA SPIRIT OF EASTER ISLAND** 93

Makemake the Dwarf Planet 94

How Makemake was given his unusual name 94

The Story of Easter Island 95

The Island's different names 98

History of the Islanders 99

The outstanding seamanship and astronomy of the ancient Polynesians 99

The Island's timeline 102

Stories of the Islands first Polynesians settlers 103

A record of the first contact and the terrible outcome 104

The next 140 years were no better 104

The sexual freedom of the Islanders 105

The holocaust that decimated and killed the population 107

What was left of old Easter Island and Makemake 108

William Thompson's Report for the National Museum 1891 109

Taboo and Mana 110

The Islander's spiritual beliefs 111

Ancient spiritual hieroglyphs called Rongorongo 112

Longevity, herbs and the mysterious Lomi-lomi healing method 114

The festival of the sea-birds eggs 115

Tricksters and thieves 118

The stone giants 119

Where does the god Makemake come from and what does he represent? 122

What does Makemake look like? 126

The Meaning of Makemake to the Islanders 128

Makemake, the Great Sea Spirit 128

Makemake as a sexually bawdy deity 129

Physical prowess and competition 131

Birds as sacred beings and messengers of the divine 131

The magic of shells and feathers 132

How Will Makemake Help us in the 21st Century? 133

Eastern spiritual beliefs 133

Our exploration of the cosmos and a gung-ho, seafaring spirit 134

The theme of duality that occurs throughout all Kuiper Belt planets 134

Rabbits and more rabbits! 135

Makemake brings abundance. Illusion or not? 136

Comparison of the microcosm of Easter Island to the macrocosm of planet Earth. Over population and de-population 137

Makemake and pandemics 139

Has the Great Sea Spirit returned to guide us into proper use of the seas again? 139

Chapter 7 **HAUMEA, GODDESS OF HAWAII, BIRTH, NATURE, ROCK AND FIRE** 141

Haumea the dwarf planet and the dispute in which two men claimed her 141

Why the name Haumea was chosen 142

President Obama and a Hawaiian planet 143

Peculiar features of the planet 143

Haumea, the Goddess of Hawaiian Myth 144

Hawaiian creation chant 144

Haumea as goddess of fertility in wild plants and forest 145

Haumea as goddess of childbirth and Fire 146

The layers of the Multiverse compared to Hawaiian culture 146

What Does Haumea Represent in the 21st Century? 147

Haumea rules natural cycles such as those of the Moon 147

Circadian rhythms and breast cancer 148

Hawaiian spiritual concept has now been proven scientifically 149

Haumea as nature and sacred Earth 150

Chapter 8 **ERIS, GODDESS OF STRIFE, STIMULATION AND RIVALRY** 151

The discovery of Eris, thought to be the tenth planet 151

A religious cult called Discordianism 154

The mythology of Eris 154

A goddess who represents the natural law of Fire and the chaos of the Godness 155

The positive side of Eris in myth 156

Using Hesiod to Understand How to Engage With Eris Energy in the Most Positive Way 156

Living life to take advantage of Eris's competitiveness 156

Good Eris as part of the natural justice system 157

Some final thoughts on Eris 158

Chapter 9 SEDNA. THE PRIDE AND OUTRAGE OF THE GREAT OCEAN GODDESS 161

Sedna, a strange new `planet` 162

The Myth of Sedna 163

What does Sedna's myth mean to the Inuit people? 165

Sedna and the Shaman 165

Primal force of nature and stroppy red head 166

Animals and humans are interchangeable 167

What Does Sedna Mean Now? 167

History of global warming and retreating ice in the Polar Regions 168

Global warming and retreating ice now 169

"The Inconvenient Truth" and the International Polar Year Initiative 170

Sedna the planet could be used to predict the storms and floods 171

The tsunami of 2004 and the sinking of Atlantis 172

Hurricane Katrina 173

The bird flu pandemic and the spirituality of birds 174

The Great Cycles 175

Evidence that we have done all this before? 177

What Can We Do? 178

On a global level 178

On a spiritual level 179

On a personal level 180

Chapter 10 WHAT DOES THIS MEAN FOR US IN THE BUS QUEUE? 183

Where are we going with all of this? What's going to happen this century? What's going to happen to our children? Or even "in the End"?

The doom, gloom, worst case scenario bit 183

The Gold, Silver and Lead Races 185

Reaching for Something Bigger 186

The fears and difficulties of reaching for 'bigger' 186

So what might 'The bigger picture' be about? 188

Looking at earthly concerns and possible remedies 189

The something we have in the 4% that absolutely ensures our future 190

Human worship is needed to feed the Spirit of the 96% 191

World religion and religious dynasties 192

"The Key" from the Hermetic Texts and the key to it all 193

REFERENCES FOR ALL CHAPTERS 197

Endnotes and credits for illustrations 210

Credits for cover images 211

Chapter One

"We shall not cease from exploration.
And the end of all our exploring
Will be to arrive where we started.
And know the place for the first time."
- T.S. Elliot.

CHANGES ARE HAPPENING

Lo!…There is a Star in the East….

Two thousand years ago 3 astrologers rode into Jerusalem on camels and announced that a new star in the East heralded the birth of a Messiah. This remains one of the most famous translation jobs done by astrologers, and hopefully, this book follows in that tradition!

The story this time revolves around the discovery of new planets in our solar system, and the re-classifying of others. These changes herald a transformation of 2,000 years of spiritual understanding and patriarchal domination. History is being written, and something very special is happening.

Ok, so what's a solar system?

It's a load of planets and objects revolving around a sun. Each star in the sky is a sun, so as you can imagine, there are rather a lot of solar systems! When we speak of *the* solar system, we mean ours. In the last 2,000 years, knowledge of our solar system has had 2 periods of considerable change; the first starting in 1610 and the second one at the beginning of the 21st century. The first one coincided with the arrival of the modern era and major scientific, industrial and cultural revolution.

The one we are in now saw a sudden explosion of discoveries from 2004 onwards.

This book takes six of the recent planetary discoveries and changes to the solar system and explains what these mean to the human race and on a personal level. Meaning is drawn from the myths surrounding the planet's name, the events surrounding it's discovery and an in-depth knowledge of astrology. (But not using any astrology jargon.)

How Can Changes to the Solar System Convey New Spiritual Meaning?

Strange as it may sound, 'BIG' finds in astronomy always coincide with major shifts in the evolution of the human race and spiritual understanding. And when I say 'changes to the solar system', I need to make it clear that these are really big changes!

The last really big change in our understanding of our solar system began in the 17th century, when Galileo devised an astronomical telescope and was locked up for finding the moons of Jupiter and daring to state that the Earth *wasn't* the centre of the Universe……. *and* it revolved around the Sun.[1] He also discovered Neptune at this time, but was so excited by the Jupiter's moons, he did not even register Neptune as a planet.[2] Other fundamental discoveries included working out why our Moon hadn't fallen to Earth, and the mathematical calculations that allowed the discoveries of more planets. Galileo published a book about his discoveries called The Starry Messenger and this book is so titled to honour the name of this great astrologer. (He was both a scientist and an astrologer.)

The centre of the civilised world shifted from Italy and the rigidly dogmatic Catholic church, to Northern Europe. Isaac Newton and the new Republic of England heaved themselves out of the grip of the Middle Ages and a scientific revolution began.[3] As Uranus and Neptune were discovered, revolutions of all kinds were in full swing.

So, what's happening these days? Read any holistic or spiritual magazine published in the early years of the 21st century and you are told of "Changes to Earth Consciousness" and "Ascendance to Higher Dimensions". People who listen to angels and go to the local Reiki night were whispering of awakenings. From Leighton Buzzard to Newcastle-under-Lyme, whilst we slept and gossiped at the school gate, something was stirring.

From 2003 a great many things were stirring in the world of science and quantum physics too, phenomenal discoveries and theories were emerging. But the jargon was so hard to understand and explain, that the journalists and public gave a yawn and turned to the sports page.

Changes are certainly happening with regard to the Earth's climate and even Earth the planet is changing……..the magnetic core has started to gallop to a different North.[4] But fortunately, global navigation satellite systems mean we don't have to rely on magnetic compasses any more, so getting lost won't be a feature of the future.

It seems that when we make breakthroughs in knowledge in *any* sphere of life, all other areas grow and change too, even if they seem unrelated, nothing gets left behind. And *really* big breakthroughs…..`coincide` with *really* big breakthroughs.

In astrology, the recent changes to our known solar system will hold strong signposts and clues about the years to come, since these energies will become a feature of our lives as they walk side by side with us. The meanings, myths and circumstances surrounding the discovery and naming of these new planets or objects will forever be what this planet symbolises. Both personally, and in the collective. The name is particularly important, since they always choose names of deities (gods and goddesses) from mythology. After the name is announced we have all those mythological stories to tell us of that planet's meaning.

That fact is probably the most unbelievable in astrology, because astro***nomers*** name planets. And an astronomer is different to an astrologer. An astronomer is a scientist who measures the heavens using complicated mathematical formulae and associated complex instruments; he does **not** believe that they convey meaning. An astro***loger*** is spiritually motivated and associates behaviour and meaning with a planet. Astrologers know that the planets affect the Earth, the human race, and every single human being. The planets symbolise energies that influence us.

So how come a lonely astro***nomer***, sitting on some deserted mountaintop in the middle of no-where with a telescope, happens to pick the right name? The answer is mysterious, magical and possibly to do with the hidden hand of the Divine but the scientist would never accept that. It is my opinion that the scientist astronomer is under the influence of the planet and the planet, therefore, `tells` the discoverer what to call it. He would have been studying it and looking at it for so long, he would have become immersed in it's energy and meaning. Mike Brown, the astronomer in charge of the team that discovered most of the dwarf planets which form the basis of this book, said of one of them, Eris, that she behaved so like her mythological character that it almost made him believe in astrology.[5]

Another influence on the astronomer is the current collective issues, fashion and general feelings at the `eureka` moment. As cut off as the astronomer might be, he is still connected to these influences spiritually, through the Ether. The moment that he gives the planet a name, he acts as spokesperson or becomes the mouthpiece for the unseen cosmic web of connected energy.

How Our Knowledge of the Solar System has Changed

If we go back thousands of years B.C., it is more than likely that the iconic great civilisations knew much more than we do now about astrology and our solar system. For some reason the coming of one-god-religion brought about a **de**-volution of this knowledge. We went backwards and lost or devolved knowledge. Massive libraries of ancient superior knowledge were burnt, and many great secrets of the Universe were lost forever. We have a few scraps and hints, but we haven't regained enough intellectual, technological and spiritual ground to understand what the scraps and hints mean! Although we do seem to be shifting some ground recently. (The trouble is, we are mainly in the hands of archaeologists, and these guys spend so much time looking down at sand and clay their thinking turns to concrete, their necks get stuck in the one position, and unfortunately they find it difficult to look up and be inspired by the stars. Sorry guys!)

The model of the solar system from around year 01A.D. to about 1610A.D. didn't change much. It consisted of all the planets we can see with the naked eye, with the Earth in the middle.

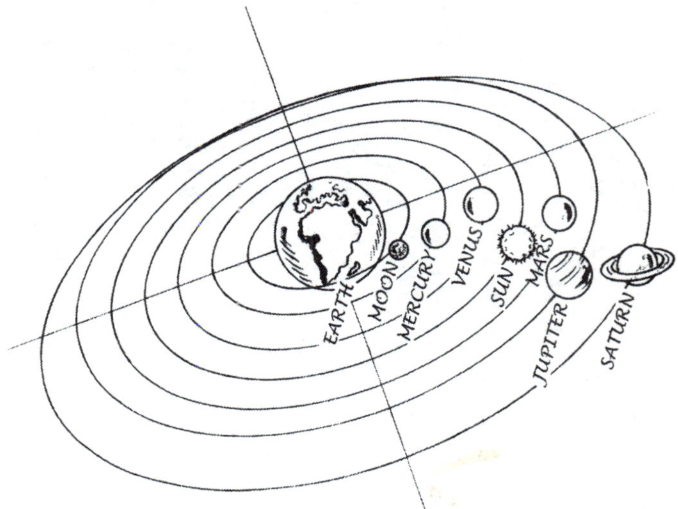

Illustration 1. *How the solar system was thought to look until 17th Century.*

This hopelessly wrong image of our solar system, with the 'flat' Earth at the centre of the Universe, quite literally demonstrated how very intellectually and spiritually restricted the human race was. Cultural growth was relatively limited, and our knowledge of the solar system reflected this. Saturn was the limit of the planets that were known, (the is the outermost planet that can be seen with the naked eye) and he represented the limit placed on growth and evolution.

In astrology, those innermost planets represent those parts of our personality that we most recognise and control. Our overall ego, our emotional vulnerability, how we communicate, how and what we desire and value and the energy we use to get all that. The outermost two, Jupiter and Saturn, represent growth and restriction. That was all we needed to know. Ourselves, and what restricted us.

It is interesting to note that this patriarchal time had 2 feminine planets and 5 masculine ones, reflecting the bias towards the masculine.

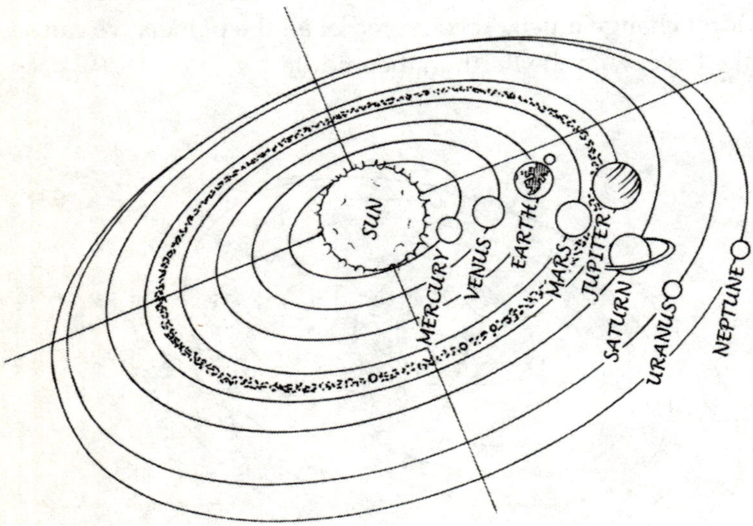

Illustration 2. *The solar system after 1849.*

Next we see the solar system after 1849. The Sun is now at the centre, two planets have been added to the outer edge, and an asteroid belt of smaller objects is now known to exist between Mars and Jupiter

Ok, so at least we now have things in the right order. The discovery of Uranus and Neptune symbolised the beginning of a cosmic or bigger world-view. Universal energies were now coming into play and we would start to see the human race as part of a much bigger plan or cosmos.

The asteroids were generally ignored until the recent big change. There was a flurry of scientific data as they were discovered around 1800, then they sunk into obscurity, and were ignored. It's as if it just wasn't the right time. Strangely the 4 biggest asteroids were all named after goddesses so they represented feminine energy. Perhaps it wasn't the right time because the world wasn't ready to pay homage to matriarchal again. Now, one of them is part of the new changes, and this recognition has coincided with the re-emergence of the feminine or goddess universal energies once more.

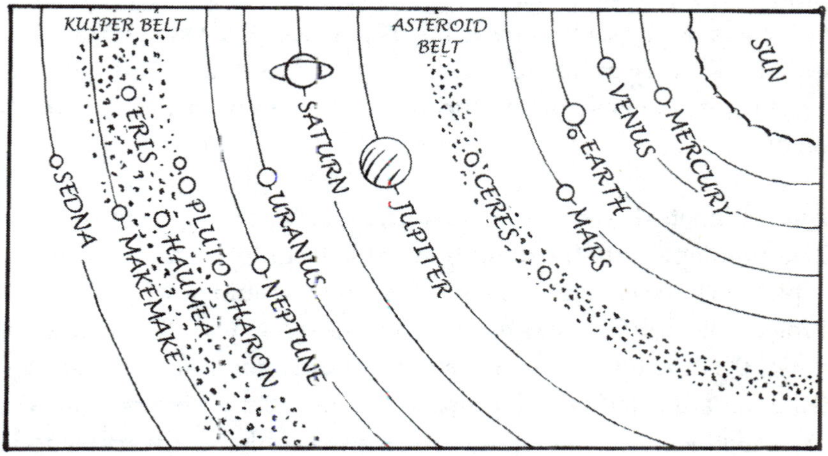

Illustration 3. *The latest re-organisation of the solar system for the 21st century*

In this illustration you will see the addition of Pluto-Charon, Eris, Makemake, Haumea and Sedna in the outer reaches of the solar system, and the recently acknowledged and promoted dwarf planet Ceres, that was already within the asteroid belt of the old solar system, but ignored. This organisation was formally announced in August 2006.

The Discovery of a Whole New Region of the Solar System

The discoveries in the outer reaches of the solar system were partly made possible because of more sophisticated instruments, but also because the astronomers started looking in a different part of the sky. All the known planets in earlier times were all spinning around the Sun in a straight line, or on a flat plane. Like looking at a plate from side on. So they made the assumption that any other planets farther out would also be along this plane. Pluto, discovered in 1930, was the odd ball. He wasn't in a line with all the others, he was at an angle to it. So he was the first messenger to tell us there was more. He seemed to say, "Don't follow the same old line of thinking, step outside of your safe, known boundaries". So they eventually did. They started to look elsewhere…and they found lots! A far out doughnut shaped ring around the solar system called the Kuiper Belt, which comprises of many objects and rocks; some as big as planets. They symbolise a new world of discovery in the fields of science and technical stuff, plus the expected spiritual growth and future experiences of the human race or collective.

The new planets discovered in the outer reaches of our solar system caused problems with the definition of the term `planet`. Were all the new planets to be called `planets`? If so, they would have to keep re-writing all the school books every time a new one was discovered. In August 2006, the International Astronomical Union (the scientists) got together and decided on a definition that meant anything new would not be called a planet; it would most likely be called a `dwarf planet` instead. The only trouble was, this new definition would have to apply to Pluto….so Pluto could no longer be called a planet and he was demoted to `dwarf planet` status. There was press and public outcry, letters were written to the Times and people went into mourning. Arguments and bust-ups abounded in the usually stuffy world of astronomy as the scientists argued about who had discovered what….and what it should be called. One of the new planets was named after the Greek goddess of strife and rivalry, so that was pretty apt!

The new discoveries were given the names of god/desses from ancient world civilisations as far apart as Iceland, Greece and Polynesia. The mythology surrounding each of them tells us about the things that will become important to the human race in the 21st century. Sedna speaks of climate change, huge global movements of water and the plight of sea creatures. Pluto-Charon symbolise nuclear energy and scientific breakthroughs in sub-atomic physics that will reveal other, invisible dimensions. These other dimensions of science will prove to include the mythical Underworld of our ancient spiritual texts. Makemake represents pandemics and over population, but also changes in religion and spiritual beliefs. Haumea, another Polynesian deity, also represents new spiritual understanding with clearer understanding of our origins, fertility and creation. Ceres will also alter our attitude to death and the soul's passage into other dimensions. Another of her spheres is farming and she will be needed to help us manage world crops, food security and shortages. This just leaves Eris, who represents the choice between strife and rivalry or ethics, natural justice and determined endeavour.

We Will Discover What Our World Was Created From, Why and How

Put very simply, Earth/matter/order is created from Fire/spirit/chaos. Energy takes on form and becomes matter. This is called the Big Bang in science, or the `Fall` in orthodox religion.[6] Our world was created out of another that is pure energy, a formless soup of divine potential – the god/desses. We will come to understand more of the mighty, invisible forces or deity controlling this delicate balance. The new planets speak of our ability to find answers to the deeply hidden, invisible forces and our understanding of the spiritual energies that underpin our world will expand as rapidly as our science. The scientists call it `dark` matter and `dark` energy. Dark simply means invisible, or in another dimension, something completely undetectable. We will discover amongst other things, the `Underworld`. The stories of burning hell fires and purgatory of the Roman Catholic Church were based on their worst earthly experiences, which were the volcanoes of Italy. Civilisations will always use the images around them to understand the spiritual. It is time to change that image, since we now have a much bigger Cosmos to look at and not just a region of Earth.

We will also be pushed into greater responsibility for physical Earth - raw materials, food, crops and nature. Mother Nature and the primordial feminine or matriarch is re-emerging.

Well that's a quick over view of their meaning, but now it's time to see what each of these separate new energies is about in detail……..

"The entire Universe is this gigantic loaf with many other slices, potentially. So our Universe could be one slice, and a different parallel Universe could be living on a different slice."

- Brian Greene, Physicist.

COOL SCIENCE

Before we look at what some of the new planets are symbolizing it would be helpful to try to understand the new realms that science is discovering. As we saw in the first chapter, the two things are linked and some of the new planets are describing these new realms. I have tried to make this chapter really simple, but in truth the new scientific discoveries are mind-boggling and awesome. If you do find it a bit difficult to take in all at once, just go to the back of this chapter where I have written an explanation simple enough for my mother to understand. That will be enough for you to fathom the rest of the book.

Why Are We Making All These Discoveries Now?

Science now has super powerful instruments that can see things one millionth the size of a speck of dust and it is revealing things stranger than even science fiction could imagine. It is called quantum physics or particle physics, since the tiniest bits of all are called `particles`.

Likewise, there have been big improvements in space telescopes. Some have been launched into orbit around the Earth and these can see the stars much more clearly than before. This has led to big leaps in our understanding of the Universe, although each leap gives us more questions than answers. One of the most wondrous things to behold is how science, spiritual beliefs and mythology are all converging. However, it has to be said that it is scientific understanding that is changing most and revealing realities that make complete sense of ancient spiritual texts written thousands of years ago. The academic community previously discounted these texts as gibberish. Scientists and spiritual intellectuals will deny this converging of opinion furiously, since neither is keen to be associated with an enemy previously thought to be un-enlightened. However, the similarities between them just grow every day. This will become obvious as you read through this book

What is Matter? What is Our Universe Made Of?

Everything that you see around you, the chairs and furniture in the room, this book, your body and even the water vapour that you exhale, can all be broken down into smaller and smaller bits. The chair is made of wood, wood is made of cells, the cells have molecules, and the molecules are made of atoms. And for hundreds of years - up until the 20th century - that was it. It was thought that the atoms were the hard bits that gave matter, or wood, it's rigidity, so that when you touched it, it felt hard. And when microscopes were invented that could measure the really tiny, the scientists assumed that they were on the verge of looking inside the solid bit.

But they looked right through the atom and still they couldn't find much of a solid bit! Atoms are almost empty caverns. There is a bit at the centre called a nucleus.......*but*.... the nucleus in the atom has the same proportions as a fly in a cathedral! That's a lot of empty space.[1] The nucleus is made up of `particles`, hence the name particle physics.

There are bits that whizz around the nucleus and these are called electrons, but these aren't solid either. They are described as "weird excitations and vibrations of invisible field energy"[2] Whatever that means....it doesn't mean solid bits!

Put simply, it's like the spokes of a bicycle wheel that look solid when the wheel is spinning really fast. They would even feel quite solid if you were to stroke them with a feather, but when the wheel stops the spokes don't add up to much at all, and now the feather can easily pass through unperturbed.

The spinning bits of energy have organised themselves into a `lattice` that holds together and repels things or feels resistant to the touch. So when your finger touches your arm, both feel solid. This illusion of solidness is in all matter and every material thing in the Universe including you and me. A biologist says "Physical atoms are made up of vortices of energy that that spin and vibrate...." And they then "had to come to realize that the Universe is not made of matter suspended in empty space but energy."[3] As energy is the same thing as `spirit`, this confirms we are spiritual beings.

A Parallel Universe Or Other Dimension That Supports Ours

But it's even weirder than that. They occasionally see particles that just appear and then disappear. They pop in and out of what has to be another invisible dimension - a parallel reality. Yep, really, a parallel reality! Another dimension that is `stuck` to the underside of ours. This has got to be like material that has gold thread woven into it that you can only see from one side. From our side we can't see the gold thread, but it is there, silently giving extra weight and support to the fabric. This invisible, unknown dimension might be like a giant spider's web that we can't see, but it extends out into the universe connecting everything up. A little vibration at one end will send a rustle of energy down the web to all the other parts. So you put your toaster on, and somewhere out in the Cosmos, someone could know.

According to Science, You Have a Dark Super-Body

There has to be something that gives matter it's bulk and weight – it's `mass`. But according to physicists, the mass of the nucleus of an atom is far heavier that the sum of all its particles. That means…….. add up all the bits and the total is more than it should be – a lot more than it should be! According to one Nobel Prize winner, Frank Wilczek, 95% more than it should be.[4] That is an amazing statement – 95% of an atom is missing. We can only find or see 5%. To explain this, there is a popular theory that says for every particle of matter in an atom there is an invisible particle - a particle of `dark` matter called a `super` partner.[5] All that seemingly empty space does have something in it that has mass or weight, but it is `dark`. Dark means it's invisible. But not just invisible, it means we can't touch it, or see it, or interact with it. It doesn't weigh anything on our scales, it can't be measured with any scientific instruments that we've invented so far. And here's the really cool bit – because air is made up of atoms - and the particles in atoms have the dark super-partners - it's all around you now! Wave your hands around in front of you (go on, no-one's looking!) and your hands are passing straight through it. It's right there with us, but we have no idea that it is, because it doesn't register with our senses. Cool or what?

This also means that you too have a `dark` body, as well as the one you know about! (Well, we could all do with a `super-body`!)

We know that we all have a mind, body, soul and spirit. Well, science is now proving the existence of our mind, soul and spirit. The 4% is our body and 96% is our soul and spirit, which exists mostly in other dimensions; ones that are `dark` or invisible to our material body. Mind is in both - conscious is in the 4% and unconscious in the 96%.

What is The God Particle?

There is one theory about a certain particle called a Higgs boson or Higgs particle that has captured the attention of many physicists, and it is believed that it may be responsible for much of the missing dark matter. It is named after an un-assuming chap called Peter Higgs who was born in Newcastle Upon Tyne in 1929. (Same year as my Dad!) He wrote a physics papers in 1964 in which he theorized about the existence of a `dark` energetic field pervading the Universe which drags on our real particles with it's own `dark` particle – called the Higgs particle. When the Higgs particle drags on the particles in our atoms, it gives them the extra dark mass that we can't find.

For several years he was derided by his colleagues, but eventually the idea caught on and became the basis for lots of further development. However, it turned out that his career had peaked with that theory and he withdrew from cutting edge physics after that. He says "Because I'd written an influential paper, people tended to assume I understood far more about the subsequent theory than I did and I found it increasingly hard to keep up."[6] (I love that comment. The man has a Gemini Sun, and this is fairly typical. Gemini's are great at gathering knowledge but often derive no meaning from it.) The press dubbed the Higgs Boson the `God` particle, but Higgs himself dislikes the term `God` because he doesn't want to upset those who are religious.

A Nine Billion Dollar Experiment Called The Large Hadron Collider

In order to get to the bottom of all this, scientists from all over the world are working on the most ambitious experiment the human race has ever taken on. More ambitious even, than landing on the Moon As I write this, we are witnessing the launch of a project involving the largest machine ever built, called the Large Hadron Collider (L.H.C.), and it's mission is to discover the Higgs particle, or any of the tiny, invisible particles of energy that may inform us of parallel universes and other dimensions. They have to find the dark particles in an atom, or the dark energy field and properly understand them. Scientists have caught tantalizing glimpses of them in previous experiments in smaller machines, but now, paradoxically, to see even smaller, they need an even bigger machine!

The L.H.C. is a circular tunnel with a huge 27km long tube inside it, within which they can whizz beams of particles round and round. It is buried deep underground on the borders of France and Switzerland, near Geneva. It uses up so much power - about 10% of that used by the Geneva area - they can't run it over the Christmas holidays because it might compromise the power supply to the French as they cook their turkeys and open their presents.[7]

To find the dark particles, they send beams of energy with particles of `real` matter in them whizzing round inside the circular tube at the speed of light. After they have one beam behaving itself and whizzing nicely round and round, they then send another in the opposite direction and when all is going well, they slam them into each other and large detectors measure the energy that is produced by the collision. Apparently measuring the energy that is released, tells them about the dark particles that were present. (There is a bigger dying energy signature than can be accounted for by the real matter.)

This may seem like a lot of trouble to go to, but otherwise they would have to hang around waiting for these dark particles to pop in and out of our existence randomly, as they often do, but like buses, the little buggers just won't turn up when expected!

Some of the statistics involving the L.H.C. are mind-boggling. It involves scientists and support staff from 111 countries. It weighs 38,000 tonnes and it's initial construction and manufacturing costs amounted to £3.5 billion. The beams of particles will travel at 11,000 circuits per **second**. The detectors in the ring are so sensitive they can feel the movement of the Moon going overhead as it's gravitational pull sucks the water in the earth around the ring towards it. (This is through up to100 meters of rock!) And lastly, part of it will probably be the coldest place in the Universe, at absolute zero degrees.[8]

Most of the Matter out in Space is Missing Too

And then it gets *really* interesting when we look at the matter out in the Universe, because dark and invisible happens on a much bigger scale too. The fact is that 96% of the known universe is missing and is made up of dark stuff also.

Our Sun is one of at least100 billion suns, all orbiting around a centre. This is called a galaxy, and our galaxy is called the Milky Way. When the scientists do the calculations to predict how much matter (suns, planets, clouds of gas) there should be in the galaxy to stop it all flying apart, there is a load missing. In fact, not just a load missing - most of it is missing! In all a staggering 96% of the Universe is missing and called `dark`.

Let me just repeat that because it's just too amazing to get when it's first said! When they add up the expected mass in the Universe - when they include all the galaxies, all the suns, all the planets and big clouds of gas and debris that exist in outer space; our Earth, you and me and your cat – everything……… 96% of it is missing!

So just to sum up what we've got so far, 95% of an atom is `missing` and 96% of the Universe is `missing`. These two figures are close enough for us to assume that it is the same stuff that is missing or `dark` in the very tiny (the microcosm) and the very big (the macrocosm).

Dark Matter in the Universe.

As far as the Universe goes, the experts have broken that down further and stated that of the missing 96%, about 21% is missing dark matter, and 75% is missing dark energy. The remaining 4% is our Universe as we know it - all the stars, galaxies, planets, Earth, you and me, the other 6 billion and *everything* ……… is only 4%. The rest is an unknown multiverse or dimension with maybe even 11 other universes or dimensions in it.

So, as far as the Universe is concerned two things are `dark`. There is dark **matter** and dark **energy**. Dark matter accounts for 21% of the Universe and for starters it is everywhere you find real matter (your body, the Earth, the stars, etc.). It gathers around it in clumps. But it also stretches out into long filaments that cross the Universe and connect up stars and planets and galaxies in a supergiant `cobweb`. We have only just got the futuristic instruments that can detect this stuff, and it's early days, but courtesy of all the high tech gismos, they have actually produced images of the stuff that you can find on the Internet. If you can't be bothered, I'll just tell you it looks exactly like cobwebs. The very latest research from an eminent scientist in the field says this:

> "The vacuum is not empty. We used to think that the vacuum was empty, and that objects were things in empty space. However, the vacuum is not empty. It is a medium…… We are

like the fishes in the ocean who regard water as empty space." He also states that there may be up to 11 other dimensions and different worlds.[9]

And before you suggest that he needs to take more water with it...... he's not alone. One scientist at Fermilab has said: "There are even serious suggestions that new dimensions of space may be opening up."

Dark Energy in the Universe

So what's dark energy? God knows! And he's currently not telling. All the scientists know is that it is pretty evenly spread throughout the Universe. So there is as much in your bedroom as there is on the other side of our Galaxy. And it seems responsible for the fact that the Universe is still `growing` like a soufflé. Our galaxy is expanding at a rate of 80 kilometres per second.

The Dark Part of Our Own Bodies, Our Soul and Spirit, Gets Messages From the 96%

It seems that science now agrees with the spiritual belief that messages come to us from out of the 96%

According to a scientist, all the cells in our body are constantly receiving information from a higher organizing authority or power, and some of it may come from the invisible web of connectedness. He says that the cells in our body have an inbuilt receptive ability and they are also affected by changes in the electromagnetic waves around us.[10]

Another one agrees with him. According to a Dr. Bruce Lipton, biologist at the University of Wisconsin.

> "Hundreds of scientific studies…reveal that `invisible forces` of the electromagnetic spectrum profoundly impact every facet of biological regulation."[11]

He says that that living organisms must receive signals in order to stay alive and that "Specific frequencies and patterns of electromagnetic radiation regulate…all cellular behavior that contributes to the unfolding of life."

Apparently these energy signals are a 100 time more effective that the chemical ones that our real body relies on, such as the immune system or the endocrine system. This means that the energy that you invoke during Reiki can be one 100 times more effective than the bodies own healing system! He states that our beliefs and the energy waves we create in our thoughts create positive or negative responses. In other words if we believe in something, this has an influence over our control of it. So if you and the patient believe in your power to heal, then your healing will be 100 times more effective!

It is also known that a vast amount of nuclear power pours out of the Sun and passes through our planet and bodies constantly. The power comes in the form of quantum particles and some of these are called neutrinos. Billions and billions of them are passing undetected through our bodies all the time and it can take as little as 8 minutes to get from the Sun to our planet. The Sun doesn`t just warm our bodies, it supplies an unseen spiritual sustenance. So we are all held together by an unknown energy or force that constantly feeds us with millions of signals. It is tempting to see this as being divine in nature. Almost certainly it comes out of the 96% and the elements of Fire and Water are involved. In spiritual terms, we have ancient texts telling us that powerful forces guide us, and everything on this planet. These used to be called god/desses and in my world, such planets as Jupiter and the Sun represent them.

Some people are more connected to the invisible 96% than others. These are the people who feel psychic in some cases, or in others just get `gut` feelings that pay off with lucky events. Mediums and clairvoyants must all get their information from these other realms. Children are especially connected but as they get older they can tune it out. Ancient Hermetic texts talk of a silvery thread that connects a baby to the other realms and doesn't always get broken at the time of birth. It can remain connected for some time as the soul make a decision to stay or return, or perhaps the soul needs the continued support of the soul lake in the 96% for a while after birth. Eventually though, the thread is broken and the baby is `earthed`.

An Explanation Simple Enough For My Mother to Understand

If you found some of that heavy going, then don't worry about it. It took me 2 years to get to grips with it. You can always re-read it when you've read the rest of the book. In the meantime here is a simple explanation that will do for now, but probably wouldn't pass as very scientific:

Science has discovered that all the things we think are solid…aren't! If you took a tiny cell from your arm and magnified it more and more, you would not find a solid bit and the microscope would pass right through your arm. It looks solid and feels solid when it's all put together, but it's actually trillions of bits of spinning energy that gives the illusion of being solid. Like the spokes of a bicycle wheel that look solid when they are spinning, but allow you to see straight through when they have stopped. The spinning bits of energy in your arm have formed into a `lattice` that holds together and repels things or feels resistant to touch. So when something touches it, both things feel solid. You are actually made entirely of energy and so is everything in the world around you.

The next important thing to know is that most of the Universe is `missing` and here is a simple explanation for that.

Gravity pulls everything towards matter and holds on to it. Like the Earth holds on to us and the apple falls to the Earth. Gravity comes from matter or solidness and the Earth is a big solid lump so it has gravity which pulls us all into the centre. When they worked out how much solid stuff there would have to be in the Universe to keep everything in it's place and stop it flying apart, they were puzzled to find that most of it is missing. In fact, 96% is missing. It is there, but it is invisible to touch or measurement and we walk right through it as if it weren't there. The scientists call it `dark`.

Everything that we know in our lives, all the planets, the Sun, the stars, our Earth and everything on it including you, me and the cat….we only add up to 4% of the Universe.

This dark 96% has other invisible realms in it that are in a different dimension. We can't pass into these other dimensions because our bodies are not vibrating at the right frequency, but other things such as magical healing power, spiritual guides and angels can.

We know we each have mind, body, soul and spirit. Our physical bodies are made of the matter of the 4%, whilst the rest of us is the spiritual or etheric parts of our personality that exists in the 96%. The soul and spirit in each of us move and exist in these other realms and this is how we can `just know` things in our gut, communicate through psychic awareness, or `read` cards.

These other realms contain things that we became frightened of in the last 2,000 years but this is because we believed the horror stories of burning hell and purgatory told by the Catholic Church. They got the idea from volcanoes and it's not really like that at all. The ancient races that existed more than 4,000 years ago knew of and respected the other realms. To them they were simply the realms of the sky gods and the Underworld or Netherworld which was where the Sun went at night.

As amazing as all that sounds it is absolutely true. Proven scientific fact or theory mixed with the spiritual teachings we have always had. Each of the coming chapters will go over it again occasionally, so if you still don't understand it, don't worry because I'm sure you will by the end of the book.

Illustration 4 *Ceres*

CERES, GODDESS OF GROWING AND GRIEVING
A Great Earth Mother Goddess

Ceres the Dwarf Planet

Within the orbits of Mars and Jupiter in our solar system, there is a big wide gap that has caused speculation since the 18th century. Astronomers of the time searched for a planet that the laws of physics told them *must* be there… … but they couldn't find it! Finally, in 1801 a planet the size of Texas was discovered in the gap and called Ceres, but when other objects were also found there soon after, it was called an asteroid belt, and the newly named planet was demoted to the title of asteroid[1]. Ceres's position in the sky was no longer reported on, and the world lost interest in her. Astrologers didn't know of or use her.

Then in the 1970's someone began to plot her position in the sky again, and an astrologer wrote a book about her and the other planets in the Asteroid belt[2]. Very slowly, the astrological community was waking up from a deep sleep regarding knowledge of the goddesses (planets) that the Asteroid belt contained.

In 2006, those in charge of such matters (the International Astronomical Union) got together to decide what to call all the newly discovered planets of the 21st century, and their decision to create a new class of planets led to the surprise announcement that Ceres was big enough to join Pluto in being called a `dwarf planet`. This meant that astrologers would start to use her, and that her energy was on the rise in the collective.

Then in 2008 a report in New Scientist added fuel to the fire by suggesting that the planets Ceres and Pluto were once ONE, or at least came out of the same place. This is in spite of the fact that there is a vast distance (up to 4 billion kilometers) and 4 planets in between them! This report was mind-numbingly spooky since this is EXACTLY the case in mythology. Ceres had a daughter or younger aspect called Proserpine. Pluto makes Proserpine his queen and she rules the Underworld with him. The report, entitled "Has Pluto sent us a message in Ceres?" says:

"Does Pluto have a wayward cousin lurking in the inner solar system? The dwarf planet Ceres…..may have been born in the same realm as Pluto, but travelled all the way to the asteroid belt." [3]

Apparently the 2 planets are made out of the same stuff, and this doesn't occur anywhere else in the Solar System.

The Spiritual Meaning of Ceres

Putting it simply, Ceres represents Mother Nature, fertility, the harvest and the bond between Mother and child. The growth of a seed into maturity, and then it's separation and preparation for re-birth. This might mean the cycle of human life - from a seed – to a baby - to a maiden - to a mother; or that of agriculture and grain in particular. She is a symbol for separation and dying, and the mourning and grieving that goes with it, but she is also the energy that is with us as we prepare for re-birth, or a new beginning or a re-generation. The early civilizations believed that the human soul went through a cycle of death and rebirth just like corn does. Her myth is one of many concerning the death and re-birth of vegetation, and it exists to encourage us to believe that human life does not end in death.

Our soul is here to learn and grow, and it is a sad fact that sometimes the greatest growth comes with great pain, because usually we have to see something end or pass before we grow into something new. Pain and spiritual growth are proportional to each other. Ceres comes to us not just for the light of birth, but also for the dark of death. She takes our hand and walks with us through the Underworld of the darkest of nights, and her gentle sensitivity teaches us of our soul, and the reason for it's existence. We see and feel the intensity of a flower. She tends us while we grow.

To explore her meaning more thoroughly, we first have to look at her myths, and then the energies that were prominent in the collective when she emerged into our consciousness physically, as a newly discovered planet.

Myths take us back to the goddesses, deities or energies of pre-history. These stories are as old as time, but very valuable, because they have stubbornly survived oppressive religious or political dynasties. Some look as if they *became* the basis for religious doctrine. When we need to understand something, it helps if we can look at the patterns, themes and issues, in a context that we can understand. Because these myths have survived, we know that the human race must always have needed them, and that they must have found them rewarding. It's as if they remind us of some knowledge stored in our genes or our human DNA somewhere. They talk to or activate an ancient memory that we all carry deep inside our soul. Carl Jung, the psychiatrist, was convinced this was so.

The Myth of Demeter and Persephone

Ceres was specifically introduced by the Italians to help deal with a drought in Rome in 496B.C., but she was originally known to the Greeks as Demeter (Earth Mother[4]), and going even further back, to the Ancient Egyptians as Isis. The best and longest account of her myth is told in a song called "Homeric Hymn to Demeter" which was written in the 7th Century B.C.E. and has several translations that are all similar.

In a nutshell, the story describes the agony and mourning a mother (called Demeter in Greek or Ceres in Roman) goes through, when her daughter (called Persephone in Greek or Proserpine in Roman) is abducted and taken into the Underworld to become Queen and wife to the Lord of the Underworld. Eventually the daughter is returned because her Mother withholds all crops and food from the human Upperworld. The other gods cannot allow the human race to die, so they broker a deal that means the daughter will spend part of the year in the Underworld, and part in the Upperworld. The object of this hymn was to explain the Mysteries of life and death in an indirect way, since it was forbidden to speak of them directly.

Here is a lengthy version of the story[5] which originally used the older Greek names of Demeter and Persephone throughout, but I've changed them to Ceres and Proserpine as the Romans did, and this will save you getting confused. It's actually helpful if you can remember both names for each, then when you read anything else you will know it is the same person. (That'll impress you mates too!)

As the hymn begins, we find the two goddesses Ceres and her daughter, Proserpine, enjoying an idyllic day in a golden age of never ending abundance and growth. Proserpine's father, Zeus, had decided that his brother Pluto would make a good husband for her, so it was agreed that the earth should split open and Pluto would rise out in his golden chariot and take Proserpine back into the Underworld with him. (A golden chariot is not exactly a symbol of destitution and poverty, and Pluto did rule a third of the world, so all was not a complete disaster!) Strangely, although the Earth opened up to let Pluto abduct her, wherever he took her, Proserpine could still see the "star filled sky", the "fish-swarming sea" and the "rays of the sun", so she had hope. The poem does not say how this was possible. I think it might be important for us to reflect on this detail. From the Underworld she could still see life on earth.

On the 10th day of searching. Ceres was helped out by the goddess Hekate and the Sun god. Ceres refers to Proserpine as a "sweet young seedling" when asking of her whereabouts. This is making an important comparison between the growth of humans and plants. We can take from this that the two follow a similar cycle.

The Sun god said Pluto had taken Proserpine to "misty realms of darkness". (But then the Sun god would consider anything to be misty realms of darkness when compared to his light!) He urged Ceres to be pleased because Pluto was very high-ranking. Apparently Zeus, Poseidon and Pluto shared rulership of the known Universe. Ceres, however, was filled with grief over this. She then shunned the immortal world and decided to go and live as a human in a town in Greece called Eleusis, which is West of Athens. (It is interesting how closely interwoven the world of the immortals and the earthly mortals are. They just blend into each other in the stories. Perhaps we are meant to understand how very close to us the gods are. However, goddesses must be tall, because we are told Ceres's head touched the ceiling of rooms, although she was not recognised as a goddess.)

Ceres blessed four maidens with the wish that "you are able to bear children, in accordance with the wishes of your parents". (This is one of her main themes as a planet today, the whole area of childbirth and the parent/child bond.)

Another of her themes is expressed when we are twice told that women say to Ceres "We humans endure the gifts the gods give us, even when we are grieving over what has to be." This goddess is very much involved with the grieving process of loss.

Ceres was then given the job of nanny to a late born, much wanted and treasured son of a King. She doesn't feed him breast milk or grain, but she raises him as a god. The act of eating symbolizes engagement with the earthly realm. By not feeding, the baby does not become human.

Every night Ceres placed the boy in fire to burn any humanness from him, and this would have led to him becoming a god or divine spirit. (In astrology, fire is the symbol of spiritual understanding and deity. Ceres was feeding his soul with spirit.) The baby thrived well, started to look like a god, and would have become ageless and immortal had his mother not discovered what Ceres was doing one night.

The mother screamed in terror at seeing her child in the flames and Ceres had to take the child out of the fire and put him on the floor. Ceres was cross and said that humans were unable to recognize something fortunate. That what looked bad for now, would have become something much better had it been allowed to go on. She could have made the boy immortal, but now he was doomed to die, as all humans must. This is another important point to grasp when considering what we can learn from the energy of Ceres. Although something may look like tragic and terrible; in time and with persistence, something good can come out of it. Ceres insisted she is "greatest boon and joy for immortals and mortals alike". And that contact with her gave something of value. (However, it was only right that the young prince became human, and Ceres was forced to allow this)

Ceres then left instructions on how to perform sacred rites that would teach the secrets of life and death, (called the Eleusinian Mysteries) and they built a temple at her bidding.

Her grief and yearning for Proserpine continued and Ceres made it a terrible year for humans. The human race was near the brink of extinction and things were getting serious! If the whole human race died, then the gods would not get their worship. Humans get their vegetation courtesy of the gods, but then the gods get something back from humans. I believe that homage and adulation by humans is an act of focus that generates an energy (spirit) which then passes into the Ether and feeds the universal spirit of the 96%. The gods desperately need this worship-generated energy, and it jeopardizes their way of living if they don't get it. So Zeus intervened and instructed Pluto to let Proserpine go. Zeus assented that she should spend a third of the year underground and two-thirds in the company of Ceres and the other gods.

Ceres immediately filled the fields with a rich and bountiful harvest and all was well again. She then bestowed upon them her second great gift to the human race - The Eleusinian Mysteries – the secrets of life and death.

The Eleusinian Mysteries and Life after Death, A Guide Into the Underworld

Ceres showed the mortals how to perform certain sacred rites and rituals, which were associated with love. Whoever was initiated in these rites would "get a share of things" once they died and went into the "dank realms of mist". Once a human has seen these things they are sent "Ploutos, - wealth personified, who gives riches to mortal humans".

They became the famous Eleusinian mysteries and major `initiation` or life and death rites of the ancient world. The Greeks believed that the soul of all growing things is in the earth and that the regeneration of spring after the death of winter is like the regeneration of the human soul after death. It was the common belief in Athens and Egypt that whoever had been taught the Mysteries would, when he died, be deemed worthy of divine glory. Hence all were eager for initiation.

Since Greek society at this time was moving towards masculine or yang energy, *individual* importance and survival was becoming most important. Feminine or Yin energy, such as Ceres's, tends to sacrifice single life in the knowledge that it is part of a whole which will be ultimately protective to the whole. As society became more focused on analytical self-development, it would have been inherently natural to maintain an appreciation of Mother Nature and Ceres as a kind of opposite to the prevailing cultural trend.

Probably to maintain the sacredness and importance, the exact content of these rites has remained a mystery, but we have a few clues.

In the Hymn, Proserpine is referred to as a young seedling, and in fact the 3 goddesses named are all different manifestations or parts of the same cycle. The seed and young seedling (Proserpine), the mother plant bearing an ear of corn (Ceres), the withering plant after harvest (Hekate) and then the seed again. This can be put into human terms – human seed, embryo, baby, maiden, mother etc. These are different stages of development of the same Earthly process – life form emerging, growing and decaying. It is likely that the Mysteries explained this.

In it's simplest form, the myth explains the seasons. So when the myth talks of Ceres's mourning whilst Proserpine is underground, it could be a metaphor for Mother Nature mourning whilst the seed is underground i.e. in the Underworld. This is the time when things must rest, and go out of sight (death) before re-birth. This is the fundamental message of the Mysteries. That humans also share this cycle or pattern. Death is not a finality, it's a preparation for re-birth. Ceres's energy is all about *growth*. How one life leads to another. How this year's crop provides the seed for next years after a period in the Underworld. A seed will always promise new life. As you look at any seed you see the promise of amazing potential.

Another clue as to what happened in the Eleusinian Mysteries comes to us from pottery made around the time the hymn was written, and Ceres was introduced to Italy. A book on Athenian red figure vases[6] contains one example of a cup painted by an artist from Eleusis. This shows a male and female in an erotic act, which is apparently a rare scene for the time and may offer us some insight as to what was encouraged in the town of Eleusis!

Protector of Life and Death Cycle, Ensuring Re-Birth and Growth.

Ceres is a metaphor for Mother Nature in all her stages of growth and decay, and there is no doubt that Ceres is a symbol of life's evolution and generation through the physical process of nurturing seeds and harvests to fulfillment. Be it the human seed, as when we procreate and make a child out of the potential seed that is within us, or seeds of grain. She has very strong associations with grains of corn in particular.

But Ceres is not only representative of the life and death cycle, she *protects* it. In the myth she could not stop Pluto or the Underworld taking her progeny for a while, BUT she did influence Proserpine's return. She will simply not allow there to be no re-birth, and her power proved to be the most influential. Let's reflect on that. She could not stop the death, but she *ensured* the re-birth. Ceres's greatest gift is that of growth, which we see when Proserpine was returned. The Hymn tells us that the Earth was immediately filled with burgeoning fields of bountiful new corn. This is what she does best. She will stay with us and wail and mourn with us during the loss, but always she seeks to grow. These days, Ceres guides souls into the Underworld....but also out again.

The Freemasons state (on more than one website) that Plutarch, a famous ancient Greek philosopher and initiate, says in his `Immortality of the Soul` that the soul at the moment of death, goes through the same experiences as those who are initiated into the great mysteries. The word and act are similar: we say telentai (to die) and telestai (to be initiated).[7]

Isis the Egyptian Goddess

The myth of Isis, the Egyptian Goddess, is almost identical, with this time a young prince of Byblos being the child who is saved from mortal death by engulfing him in flames every night. When caught by the child's mother, Isis explained that she was burning away the mortal parts of the child so that he might live forever. However, the spell was broken so he would now die, as all humans must.

Isis is the wife and sister of Osiris, the mythical original King of Egypt. Their brother, Seth, wished to rule, and murdered Osiris, scattering the body parts all over Egypt. Isis repaired the body sufficiently to draw semen from it with which she impregnated herself. She cared for the child, Horus, without her husband's earthly help, and brought her fertilized egg through to his eventual position as a state god and mythical ruler of Egypt.[8]

In order to protect her son and assure his succession to the throne of Egypt, Isis had to accept that he be raised in secret by others, and so had to be separated from him for many years. Parent child separation and the parent child bond is one of her themes.

After Isis used magic to resurrect him into a god, Osiris became ruler of the Underworld and King of Eternity with Isis his Queen and Queen of the Gods. She was also called "The-Provider-of-Nourishment" and was the goddess of fertility and the harvest.

The Ancient Mysteries of Egypt

A very important event that happened around the year of Ceres's discovery was the invasion of Egypt by the army of Napoleon Bonaparte. He took with him a team of artists who published their famous work in 1801, the year of Ceres's discovery, and caused Egyptian antiquities to be `discovered` too.

Paul Brunton was a guru and spiritual man who has been credited with bringing the experience and knowledge of enlightenment and spiritual awakening to the West.

In 1936 Dr Paul Brunton wrote an extremely prophetic book[9], which offered the following insights to the Egyptian Mysteries. He believed that the `murder` of Osiris and his apparent resurrection in many of the wall paintings in the tombs of Egypt, was actually a depiction of the process of taking him into such a catatonic state that he appeared dead, but his awake and alive consciousness was in the next realm.

In the book he describes what he felt actually happened:

> "The candidate was plunged by hypnotic means, involving the use of powerful fumigants as well as mesmeric passes the length of his body, combined with the use of a magically impregnated rod, into the death-like trance wherein he was deprived of every semblance of life. Whilst the body remained inert, the soul retained it's hold by a magnetic thread, visible to the clairvoyant initiator, so that vital functions were preserved despite the complete suspension of animation. The whole purpose....was to teach the candidate that there is no death. And he was taught

> this lesson…by dying and mysteriously entering another world of being….When the allotted time of entrancement had elapsed he was re-awakened…Thus the symbolic pieces of Osiris were put together and brought back to life." (p.p. 169 to 173)

He goes on to tell us that the High Priests were so adept at hypnotism and mesmerism that they could cause cataleptic conditions where even rigor mortis seemed to set in. They knew how to keep the subjects mind awake while his body was in this state, so he experienced super or paranormal experiences that he remembered after he woke. They wrote the "Book of the Dead" as guidance for these living dead people, whose soul was being initiated into another world.

He continues:

> "Although this process of initiation bore all the outward semblance of expert hypnotism, it was something that went far beyond the entrancement methods of our modern experimenters, who tap the subconscious mind of man but who cannot make their subjects conscious of still profounder planes of existence."

A little further:

> "… there was more philosophic doctrine and secret practice for the……..spiritually educated and instructed Egyptians….the temples had special and isolated buildings for the real Mysteries, which were performed by a select number of priests called hierophants. …"

> "The greatest secrets….. depended on the degree through which they passed…In the earlier degrees …they were made aware of their human soul, pictured as a little birdman in the hieroglyphs, and they had solved the mystery of death. They learned that it was really the disappearance for one state of being, only to reappear in another; that it affected the fleshly body, but did not destroy the mind and the self. They learned, too, that the soul not only survived the destruction of its moral envelope but progressed onwards to higher spheres."

> "In the advanced degrees, they were made acquainted with the divine soul; ......they stood face to face with the Divine. They were first instructed in the true explanation of the Fall of Man from his original spiritual state. They were told the inner history of Atlantis. They were lifted up, sphere beyond sphere, until they found themselves in the same high spiritual consciousness as Man had enjoyed at the beginning."

Perhaps this was a bit much for the local peasants to take, so simple stories involving myths and gods were used. Much later, the Greeks had watered down popular plays describing something along these lines. The Ancient Egyptians wrote and painted their afterlife beliefs onto the walls of their tombs and onto papyrus. The most famous of these is the Book of the Dead.

The Egyptian Book of the Dead[10]

The Book of the Dead is a collection of the earliest spiritual and philosophical writings of humanity, and it informs us on the mysteries of life and death, and gives advice to the souls of the living dead who go there. It was written thousands of years B.C.E. and discovered in Egypt in the 1800's.

It seems to describe different `planes of existence` or `hierarchies` or `worlds` of afterlife or creation. Firstly in the creation, the great gods of the limitless primordial water and total darkness emerged out of non-existence. Then there came into being the celestial water, or celestial sky and stars, and the Duat or Underworld, in which Isis over-sees a `double gateway`. It appears we can travel to the Underworld or the Duat with help from Isis and we can return with full knowledge of many spiritual things. Although this place is close to our own plain of existence, there are other deeper realms from which we can't return. The book confirms Isis as protector of the body-soul (Ka) as opposed to the mind-soul, which is Nephthys, her sister, and states that Isis is "in charge of those who are to be examined".

There is one thing that caught my eye, and I include it only because it is amusing. In chapter 175, one god has a moan because in the existence *beyond* the underworld there is "no water, air, lovemaking, bread or beer; but (only) spirit being and contentment"…. which the Great Atum thinks he should be content with!

The Return of the Great Goddess After an Absence of Over 1,000 Years

As we have seen from all those representatives of the Great Earth Mother, from Isis to Demeter to Ceres, this is truly a significant and important concept for our world. In all those millennia and in all those great and mighty civilizations, there was always this goddess as a fundamental of life. Until the last 1,000 years or so, that is! Well, the Great Goddess is returning now and I for one am pleased to welcome her back.

Why Will Ceres be Important in the 21st Century?

How Ceres's Support will be Needed in Food Supply after 2006.

Ceres was introduced into Roman worship along with 2 other old Greek deities in 496B.C. because the Italians were suffering drought and famine, and needed some help[11]. Ceres must have been useful because 6 years later they built her temple in Greek style, with priestesses of Greek origin. She was designated a Goddess of the working or common classes, which gave her nationwide popular appeal.

Ceres the planet was originally discovered at the beginning of an agricultural revolution caused by new ploughing methods devised in the early 1800's. She has very strong associations with grain in particular.

The sudden and surprising announcement of her elevated status to dwarf planet in 2006 could only mean that her energy was going to be keenly felt and much needed after that. We started to understand just how much in 2007, when it was announced by United Nations scientists that in order to feed the world's population, we would need to grow as much food in the next 50 years as we did in the last 10,000 years! The global population will rise from 4.4 billion in 1980 to an estimated 9 billion in 2050.[12]

From 2005 it became quite common to seegardening programmes on the TV entirely devoted to the growing of vegetables rather than the previous fashion of garden makeovers, and the American president and U.K. Prime Minister, Gordon Brown made impassioned ples for people not to waste so much food.

There were food riots in third world countries as the price of staple grains such as rice trebled in a number of months. The changing climate conditions that brought about the loss of the world's food crops wa not of Ceres's doing, this was all the work of Sedna. Ceres was actually helping to reduce the impact of the worsening weather conditions, as we found out in England in 2007, when Ceres saved the potato and wheat harvest from failure due to flooding. (Ceres was introduced to Rome to assist with drought conditions, so she is obviously useful for either!)

The saving of the crops from the floods of 2007 was clearly shown in the astrology of the time. Sedna and Neptune were flooding large parts of England between them and the situation looked dire. The rain was relentless. Then slowly, planet Ceres edged in front of Sedna, standing between Sedna and the Earth and stopping Sedna's influence. Within hours the rain had stopped, the fields dried out and a miracle happened – the harvest could be brought home. The image of how Ceres did this still bring tears to my eyes, it is a shame that at the time, so few of us knew of her brave and timely protection.

Growing Babies, Child Abduction or Separation and Madeleine McCann

The terror of abduction is something that mothers in the 21st century struggle with and will identify with most readily. The abduction of Madeleine McCann from a Portuguese holiday resort in May 2007 was extremely well publicised all over the world. And no one will forget the horror, sadness and support that we all felt. Madeleine's horoscope shows a very strong connection with Ceres, and there was a very significant Ceres energy involved on the day of her abduction. During 2007 and afterwards, Kate and Gerry McCann were on a global stage, expressing all the anger, anguish, bewildered grief and mourning which Ceres suffered in the myth.

Ceres, Cycles and the Passage of Time

Ceres gives us an understanding of nature, her cycles and the passage of time…including patience!

When she was introduced to the Italian peasants, it was made most clear she was a goddess for the plebians. The daily work of the farming community all revolved around the natural calendar. There was a yearly plan and it could not be hurried. Sowing, weeding and harvesting were all at set times of the year, and this gave the working classes stability, routine and order. They had to stay with their land. This teaches patience and an acceptance of the dominance of a greater will than our own. Ceres says the 21st century is the time to re-learn this skill!

Ceres Supports Us Through Death and Bereavement

Death of a loved one is a heartbreaking sorrow which no words of mine can bring comfort to. And the terrible pain of bereavement is an awful and tragic experience. But somewhere along that wretched journey there is a place where the bereaved desperately want to know why. And maybe understanding an individual loss in the context of the great cycle of life, can in time offer some solace, as we then understand that the soul of our loved one is only out of sight for a while. They will return to live again, and this is promised to us by the presence of Ceres. Her rites show us a better way to understand what death and the Underworld is really all about. Maybe, if we understand that there will be a re-birth we can find it more bearable.

A significant difference in our culture is our fear and horror of the perceived atrocity of the Underworld. The Ancients Greeks had no such pre-occupation, or at least it is not a feature of the ceramics of the time. It was the Catholic Church that would introduce the horrors of a place of burning hell fires and purgatory. No such place existed for the ancient Greeks.

Illustration 5 *Illustration of the Underworld on a Greek Vase.*

This illustration of a vase from ancient Greece shows a one-off rare scene of the Underworld with the winged souls of the dead filling a giant container with the individual waters of knowledge from their own vessels. It is a calm and peaceful scene. A single figure is shown to right, toiling up hill with a large rock; perhaps an illustration of life, and what it took to get the waters of knowledge! According to a Professor of Archaeology[13] these black figure vases gave a valuable picture of life in Greece at the time and "the Underworld held little interest."

We live our lives enduring pain and enjoying happiness. As the Book of the Dead points out, we must drink, eat and make love. As we do this, our soul is constantly gathering experience and wisdom. When we die, our soul, spirit and mind return to their separate `homes`. The soul joins the collective soul and pours into it all the wisdom and experience it has learnt – some pour for longer than others!

Does it help the bereaved to understand the context in which their loved one has passed on? I think so. It can be understood that their death contributes to a cycle of life in which they continue to play a major role. That single life is not meaningless, it continues to have great value.

Another way of looking at this is to see Proserpine, Ceres and the old Crone as simply extensions of each other. Different stages of the same energy. There is no `individual`, and so no `individual` death. We are all connected. Life flows through the generations that are born from each other.

Pindar said "Happy is he who, having seen this, goes beneath the earth; he knows the end of life and he knows its god-sent beginning".[14]

Certainly, as the years unfold after Ceres's 2006 revival there will be a changing attitude to death and it's circumstances. The National Health Service and Marie Curie Foundation have recently launched a joint initiative to promote home deaths. They want to open up discussion between the dying and their survivors, so that fear and taboo will not prevent the death rites being as respectful and honorable as possible.

Previously, our taboo and discomfort at talking about and accepting the imminent death of a loved one, meant that their dying moments were in a resuscitation unit, far from the gentle hands of their loved ones, as medics vainly tried to hold back the inevitable tide of death. I think Ceres will slowly introduce us to the idea of letting loved ones go with dignity and peace. Home birth has become an aspiration…….now home death needs to be!

Ceres and The Parent-Child Bond, Parent-Child Issues.

In astrology, she is clearly a symbol of the parent-child bond. She is as much about the care and nurturing we give our progeny, as she is about the farmer's care and nurturing, which gives a good harvest of wheat.

In the early 21st century, it is likely that we will all experience parent/child bond issues, as Ceres makes herself known. I know of no one who hasn't already struggled with strong mother/daughter psychological issues. Issues to do with control and breaking free.

Carl Jung said[2] "Every mother contains her daughter in herself and every daughter her mother. Every woman extends backward into her mother and forward into her daughter."

This will be hard for some daughters to take on board, and yet it is true that daughters carry the epi-genes and spiritual and soul inheritance of the whole maternal family lineage. The matriarchal energy is passed on from mother to daughter, generation after generation. Yep……you *are* your mother!

A few might have experienced more profound sorrow or grief at separation from a parent or child, and for these unfortunate souls, reflection on the deeper meaning of Ceres may bring some understanding or comfort.

Other Ceres issues can include family miscommunications, Ceres-style revengeful or devouring mothers, or the isolation of being alone with a child.

Some Final Thoughts

If there is one theme that I feel is the reason for our lives here on earth, then it has to be that we should know and understand ourselves better. Unfortunately this is also one of the hardest things to achieve! It is my personal belief that the reason for pain is this - it is in our greatest pain that we achieve our greatest growth towards the goal of knowing ourselves. We wouldn't bother otherwise.

There is no greater love on earth than the love of a mother for a child. When this love takes us to our own `underworld` of death and humility whilst we are still living, then we are truly in the greatest pain known to mankind. A personal hell on earth.

Surely then, this is when the strangest of things can happen. We grow. Our soul grows. We can see and feel the intensity of a flower. We can experience a side of ourselves that would be unknowable otherwise. We see our soul, and the reason for it's existence. The darkest hour has the greatest light. And Ceres takes our hand. She walks with us and tends us in this pain. She tends us while we grow.

"To enter into the figure of Ceres means to be pursued, to be robbed,
to be raped, to fail to understand, to rage and grieve,
but then to get everything back and be born again" Carl Jung

Illustration 6 *A seated Pluto, his wife Proserpine, Hermes holding the Caduceus and a mortal.*

PLUTO, LORD OF THE INVISIBLE REALMS

So where has Pluto gone to?

You may remember an announcement in 2006 from the International Astronomical Union, saying it had demoted Pluto and he was no longer a planet in our solar system. The newspapers all cheerfully announced the end of Pluto, and the public were mystified. Where has it gone then? Well, of course the planet itself hadn't gone anywhere, but we were asked to accept that it wouldn't be *called* a `planet` anymore, it was now a dwarf planet of the Kuiper belt.

In astrology, this planet symbolises overwhelming and threatening change that challenges the old order of things and brings about evolution and transformation with power being lost or gained. So the announcement of the changes to Pluto the planet, and the response from the public, was entirely consistent with the astrological meaning of Pluto. And as a collective we reacted in the way that people usually respond when faced with the challenge that Pluto represents. Some embraced the change easily, some people felt real loss and went into mourning over it and others tried to cling to the old order and refused to acknowledge the new regime. However, the Pluto experience means that something can never go back to the way it was before, and likewise the changes to our solar system remained.

In the same way that we need to look for the silver lining when having a personal Pluto experience, we also need to look at how re-categorising the planets can pave the way for collective growth and enlightenment. If our perceptions of Pluto the planet are undergoing revelation and change, then so will the human race undergo metamorphosis and a different way of being.

In this chapter, I am going to cover what the Pluto dominated changes will be about. Putting it in a nutshell, we will gain knowledge, and we will come to FEAR less. We will fear death less, we will fear the Underworld less, we will fear magic and miracles less, we will fear the secret power of the un-conscious less, we will fear sub-atomic and nuclear power less, we will fear change less. Quite some list! But first..... we'll have to let go of some stuff! Such things as taboos and 2,000 years of brainwashing by religious dynasties. Old scientific certainties such as the molecular structure of matter and how many planets there are in the solar system will all have to go.

The Mythology and Ancient Stories of Pluto

Pluto as Ruler of the Underworld in Roman and Greek Mythology

According to Bulfinch's Mythology, Pluto and his 2 brothers ruled over 3 dominions; Jupiter (Zeus) was the father of gods and men and ruled the sky and heavens, Neptune (Poseidon) ruled the oceans, and Pluto ruled over the realms of the dead, which included the infernal regions and Tartarus. They were often referred to as the Underworld to give them a general title, and the land of the mortals was sometimes referred to as the Upperworld. Apparently, Earth and Olympus were common property.[1]

The realms of the dead could be accessed in different ways, and Pluto had a throne and a palace, which he shared with his wife, Proserpine. Pluto *regulated* the amount of souls in the different regions, and we are told in one story that he intervened to stop Aesculapius when he became so proficient at healing, he learned how to bring the dead back to life. Pluto would not allow this, only he and his queen were allowed to dictate what became of those souls who must accept the birth and death cycle and pass through the realms of the dead.

Another of Pluto's concerns was to ensure that his realm did not become exposed to the Upperworld, and he would check that it remained invisible by riding round it in his carriage. Invisibility was important.

One of the most important myths concerning Pluto is that of Ceres and Proserpine, which can be read in detail in the chapter on Ceres in this book, so I will not repeat it here.

The Story of Adam and Eve in the Christian Bible.

There is another myth I want to explore here that is not so commonly associated with Pluto, but I feel it demonstrates another facet of this energy, which we need to understand in our dealings with him. Once again, it demonstrates how innocence can never be recovered, how things *must* move on and change into something else.

It is that of Adam and Eve in the book of Genesis in the Bible.[2] We are told that God made Adam and Eve and a beautiful garden that housed, amongst other things, the Tree of Conscience. God forbade them to eat the fruit from this tree at the center of the garden, warning that it would open their eyes to right and wrong, good and bad, and the ability to distinguish between the two. They would then be doomed to die. A serpent then shows up and tempts Eve into picking the fruit and sharing it with her mate. The supernatural, powerful and `dark` realms are often symbolized by the serpent.

All this resonates very clearly with the Pluto theme and it's associated Zodiac sign of Scorpio in astrology. As with the Ceres myth, we see the intervention of Pluto energy in Eve's life causing an action that has life or death consequences and makes irrevocable changes to innocence. Sexual activity, temptation, regeneration, magic, lust, jealousy, the occult and the serpent itself are all ruled by the astrology sign of Scorpio and this story contains all of these things. But obviously, these natural laws must exist because the tree was there in the first place! If God really didn't want to run the risk of having his perfect creations at risk of contamination by the changes that this tree could cause, why have the tree there? We are told he planted the tree there. This must have been unavoidable, since it would obviously have suited him to *not* have it there. This seems to indicate that the Scorpionic power and natural law, which says all must be part of a cycle of transformation and change, is unavoidable, even by the god of the Bible.

Back to the story! The couple are banished from the garden with various punishments. Adam shall toil hard with farming, then die and be buried in the earth, and Eve shall suffer the intense pain of childbirth. (Eve means `life giving` in Hebrew.) The serpent looses his wings and is made the enemy of womankind. Why just womankind?

Well, I feel it is because the serpent represents Pluto, and Pluto is all about the procreation of the species, and how this impulse is more powerful than individual life. It dominates supremely. Because woman takes the more active role in procreation by actually having the new life grow inside her, and then giving birth to it, it is more so the woman than the man who has to tussle with the danger of childbirth, and try to maintain personal power when her offspring and husband require her to meet their needs unconditionally for many years. The Bible says that God's punishment also includes welcoming a husband's affections and his mastership over her.

The riches that can be gained from this are evident when the woman then grows very strong as a result of her ability to `take the weight`. If the traditional roles of `woman at home`, and `man out at work` are followed, as the Bible seems to indicate here, then I believe the woman learns a tremendous amount about herself (and her own mother), as she hears herself repeating the things she swore she never would when she was a child! Having children, and seeing ourselves being raised to the ground and rebuilt, which is what child rearing does, is probably the *most* important contribution to our own self-development. More than in any other important relationship, our children hold up a mirror for us to see ourselves. This is transforming.

It might be interesting to reflect for a moment on the different attitudes to sex found in the different texts upon which whole religious dynasties are based. Pluto/Scorpio is the energy in astrology that represents sex, as part of our procreation and the life and death struggle to keep our souls evolving. (Let's face it, if sex stopped, the human race wouldn't last for very long!) Although the Bible was rewritten from ancient texts that originated elsewhere in the Middle East, it changes completely some earlier document's instructions on this matter. In the Corpus Hermeticum Asclepius texts there is reference to childbirth and great it is, with the inference that *celibacy* will earn punishment by the daimones after death.

The God of the Bible, on the other hand, *promotes* celibacy and all that is chaste, pure and untouched and "good". However, Scorpio/Pluto took over in the guise of the serpent, and when Adam and Eve ate the fruit they became "evil" and took part in sexual intercourse and pleasures of the flesh. This is interesting because they now needed to.

Before they ate from the tree, they were not human, they were immortal and were going to last forever. So they didn't need sex or procreation or children, like the angels, they would not ever need to replace themselves. The fruit of the tree removed that immortality however, and their lives were then limited. So they then needed to procreate to keep the human race going.

Siva the Destroyer and Transformer

The Pluto energy of astrology has great resonance with the god Siva or Shiva of the Hindu religion, and although there is no recorded mythological connection between this god and the planet, it is just too obvious to ignore, and one or two present day astrologers have made this connection.[3] Indian mythology is complicated and I apologise if my interpretation hasn't quite captured all the nuances, but I have done my best. If ever you've got a spare decade or two, try reading the Secret Doctrine by Helen Blavatski written in 1888. She wrote extensively about the Creation, using a rich source of religious and mythical texts, and although it is very jumbled and rambling, it was way ahead of it's time and remains a stunning classic. I have extracted these few pearls: [The capitals and italics are true to the original text.]

> "Siva……is the Destroyer, as Vishnu is the preserver; and both are the regenerators of spiritual as well as of physical nature. To live as a plant, the *seed* must die. To live as a conscious entity in the Eternity, the passions and senses of man must DIE before his body does. `To live is to die and to die is to live` has been too little understood in the West. Siva, the *destroyer*, is the *creator* and the Saviour of Spiritual man, as he is the good gardener of nature."[4]

You might need to get a glass of wine and read that again! The last bit means that Siva brings an end to earthly experiences so that we focus on our spiritual side. This and other texts are also saying that everything created must also contain the energy and potential of destruction. Everything must have a beginning and an end. What came into existence must return to non-existence, or the `qualityless immensity`. This profound thought was part of their most ancient Indian texts. Putting that into the context of this discussion on Pluto, it means that what comes out of the Underworld and into the Upperworld, what is born, must eventually whither and die, with the soul returning to the Underworld.

The religious texts discussing Siva say that existence is only a stage in the expanding universe as it heads for ultimate destruction. Siva heads towards disintegration, and nothing can escape this process of destruction. He is the power of disintegration, and he alone remains in the beginning and the end.[5]

One of Siva's less aggressive titles is Lord of Sleep, and he has a huge influence over Yoga, where one tries to attain the ultimate in transcendence and peaceful stillness. The `sleep` bit is interesting, as it isn't immediately obvious how this fits in with the destroyer image. However, it becomes clearer when Helen Blavatski refers to a period of sleep, silence and inaction during the chaos of the Creation. (Apparently, the Universe remained unaltered for a period of 4,320,000,000 years. Some sleep!)

In the `Myths and Gods of India`, we are told that when things are depleted, or a human is tired, they enter into Siva, which is sleep and the changeless state. This is a joyful abode, where they can rest. Thus the everyday state of painless sleep or meditation is said to be the closest experience we can get to the peaceful non-existence of the next dimension - the place our soul will go when this human form is worn out and expired - the Underworld.

> "We fear death that is eternal sleep because of our failure to understand its significance. Man, in his world of illusion, fears death, even though it means for him liberation from bondage, all that is to be desired."[6]

Our fear of death is seen as ignorance, whilst the wise will see Siva as `auspicious` and the `ambrosia of all joy`. Apparently, entering into the highest state of Siva should be the supreme goal of the Indian Yogis.

The Rise and Rise of our Fascination with Ancient Egypt

Another civilization that had a highly developed sense of another realm that intertwined with ours was the Ancient Egyptians. An Egyptologist says this:

> "....judging solely from the decorations on the walls of their tombs, many of which show the daily activities of the Egyptians, they enjoyed life to the full: and it would seem that their preparations for death owed much to their wish to perpetuate that enjoyment."[7]

and

> "In order to reach the Afterlife, the dead had to face a perilous journey through the Duat. The Duat is sometimes translated as Hell of Hades, but these terms convey ideas that were alien to the Egyptians, and it perhaps safer to translate Duat as Underworld."[8]

The Duat was only as far away as the night, and the Sun traveled through it every night. It was just like Egypt, with the short cycle of night and day being a metaphor for the longer cycle of birth and death. Once again we are given really obvious examples of how an amazing civilization knew without doubt that there was a parallel universe that souls went to, but would definitely return from, if given specific instructions. Perhaps these instructions are like the scientific understanding or mathematical equations that we will need.

Their belief of the Underworld went a lot further than present mainstream Western thinking, where we just vaguely hope that there might be something more when we die. They totally accepted the existence of two realms, and these were represented by the obvious distinction between night and day. So they accepted that life has a `dual` nature. There are `dual` realms. There is a book, written by an enlightened Egyptologist, called Serpent in the Sky,[9] which seeks to prove that the snake or serpent, which is so prevalent in Egyptian art, is dedicated to the theme of `dual` and duality. Seth, a god associated with the Underworld is also associated with the scorpion and the serpent, strong symbolism with the Pluto theme that I am examining here. The Egyptians understood that the two worlds were intertwined, and now science has actually accepted the presence of another invisible dimension that exchanges energy with ours. They say it consists of `dark` matter and `dark` energy; a term ancient spiritual texts always used when discussing the Underworld. It seems strange to now be able to point to the recent scientific evidence of the quantum realm and state that there IS another dark dimension, intertwined with ours, the Egyptians were right all along. The scientists have proven that energy moves from the other dimension into ours and out again, so it makes complete sense to me that the human soul and spirit is able to do likewise when we die or perhaps even sleep.

Egyptian God Ptah "He Who Made All and Created the Gods"

An ancient Egyptian tablet of stone, the Shabaka stone, carved with text that may arguably have originated from the period 3100 – 2686B.C.E. gives a great deal of insight into the almighty creator god of Ptah. It is stated by an eminent Egyptologist[10] that the doctrine of Ptah came from the beginning of Egyptian history, and he is the oldest god, being the creator of everything else. The tablet is particularly interesting because it is written in an unusual back to front and mirror image way. It has very ancient glyphs, but a sophisticated grammar that does not match, leading some experts to believe that it *could* have been influenced by a very ancient master race. Whether or not we take the text on the tablet to have Atlantean origins, it has been called "the most remarkable monument of Egyptian thought which we possess."[11]

The Shabaka stone tells us that Ptah is the energy of creation and that he is everywhere and in everything, and that he is above (celestial) as well as below (terrestial). All the other gods and everything came into being at the behest of Ptah and he created the gods (energies) that are in wood, stone and all types of organic matter. (This is incredible knowledge since we now know that all matter is actually made up of tiny particles of spinning energy). Everything is content and united under him, and Mother Nature is infused with the sustenance and energy that comes out of the 2 lands which he unites.

It appears from this text and many other sources, that Egypt was once 2 separate lands, called Upper and Lower Egypt, and although this may be the case, I think this is also a metaphor for the 2 dimensions of Underworld and Upperworld. And as we will see later in this book when we look at recent scientific discoveries, I also think this is a metaphor for our dimension and a parallel invisible universe, which science has now proven exists. Apparently, Ptah holds the balance between the lands of Underworld and Upperworld, and this resonates with the much later Greek myth of Pluto, where we are told that he regulates the amount of souls in the Underworld.

Interestingly we are also told that Ptah's heart and tongue were used in the Creation. This is very unusual, as this is their way of saying that *thought* was behind the Creation. This is therefore the earliest known text that suggests that thought, or a divine intelligent plan is behind creation. That it wasn't just spontaneous combustion; there is intellectual concept underpinning life, a Universal Mind.

The Goddess Tiamat from the Sumerian Tablets of Creation.

Roughly 6,500 years ago, in the area now known as southern Iraq, a master race sprang into existence and began civilisation. They gave us writing, the wheel, incredible engineering, mathematical and scientific knowledge, sophisticated cities and law. They were called the Sumerians, and it seems they passed on their knowledge to all the great dynasties that came after them. The Greeks and the Christian Bible copied much of their literature. One of their greatest legacies is a set of baked clay tablets called The Seven Tablets of Creation or the `Enuma Elish`. This story describes an image of primordial feminine, the first Great Mother of existence or Mother Nature. Whilst she is an ***image*** of primordial feminine she is also ***the*** primordial feminine, and she is called Tiamat. It may seem strange that I am writing of a female energy to describe Pluto, but after many years of studying Pluto's effect on us, I have no doubt that Pluto can best be described as the dark feminine as opposed to the dark masculine. A few thousand years ago major civilisations started to make all the spiritual figureheads masculine, and by the time of the Greek empire around 500 B.C.E., women and the feminine were subjugated and devalued to a very low rank. Important feminine had been replaced with important masculine, but there is no reason now to continue this un-natural state of affairs. The emergence of the dwarf planets in astrology symbolises the end of this era, and the re-emergence of the feminine, so maybe god*dess* can have some of the important spiritual positions back now.

According to a translation of these clay tablets by Leonard W. King in 1902, Tiamat hath spawned monster serpents. (Note the serpent connection again.) She was "sharp of tooth and merciless of fang. With poison instead of blood she hath filled their bodies. Fierce monster-vipers she hath clothed with terror". None could withstand them, and vipers, dragons, raging hounds, mighty tempests and scorpion men are all mentioned.

All this really does give a wonderful image of savage, raging wrathful chest-beating vengeance, and if you talk to any ex-husband about his ex-wife after a Pluto transit has seen them through a vicious divorce case, he will use similar words! Like wise the rejected femme fatale in the movie `Fatal Attraction`, where she boiled the family bunny to get her own back. Some of Pluto's endings can be very vengeful and bitter with all sorts of raging jealousies and clawing, vicious attacks. This is the dark side of feminine and Pluto.

Tiamat is eventually killed by her son, a chap called Marduk, who is representative of masculine energy and the civilised human race. A metaphor for how the masculine conquered the feminine, and how humanity's civilised side has conquered our primeval one.

The Sumerian (Iraqi) Goddess called Ereshkigal.

The Sumerians also had a goddess of the Underworld called Ereshkigal, and once again some really well preserved clay tablets give us a story which is useful to us if we want to consider what the new image of Pluto is all about.

Ereshkigal has a sister called Inanna who must visit her in the Underworld, (perhaps something to do with a lover.) After passing through 7 gates and being stripped of clothing and adornment at each one, Inanna eventually kneels naked before Ereshkigal. She is then unceremoniously hung on a meat hook to die. However, a previously hatched escape plan meant that she was saved and emerged from the Underworld again with praises and thanks for Ereshkigal.

To understand this myth, we first have to understand what Inanna represents. In astrology, Inanna, (the planet Venus) represents our self-esteem and self worth. What we should seek for ourselves to give ourselves affirmation and self satisfaction - "because I'm worth it." She tells us about our choices in relationship too - what we need to give ourselves to get that `Wow` factor. What we find attractive and beautiful, how we desire someone. This is part of our personality, part of our ego.

So the myth shows us that romantic relationships can take us into our own personal Underworld, and if we take the Underworld as a metaphor for having a terrible and humbling experience, such as the loss of a loved one or relationship; then it is clear that the myth is meant to comfort us by pointing out that we can emerge from the suffering again. Although we are told at the beginning of this myth that no one ever emerges from the Underworld, it is clear they do, since Inanna does, and this gives a lesson of great value.

Having a determination to get out of the Underworld, or the effects of the loss, can make the best of our lives, and these myths promise us the riches of command, mastery and wisdom as a result. We emerge battered but triumphant, humbled but stronger. This reminds me of the saying "We don't loose when we get knocked down, we loose when we *stay* down." Pain and gain are directly proportional to each other, so the greater the pain, the greater the potential for gain, although it may not seem like it at the time!

Further evidence that this whole myth is a metaphor for humbling experiences can be found in the few images we have of Ereshkigal. She is often shown controlling a lion, which represents our ego, potency and strength (Leo in astrology). When we go into our darkest personal Underworld of hell, it is our ego and will that is being tamed.

It is humbling to think that a myth written as much as 6,000 years ago has survived to advise us that the suffering and humiliation we may receive in our darkest hours of hell-on-earth in the Underworld can be good for us. And that we may grow stronger and wiser as a result.

Ereshkigal herself is painted as a desperate, lonely and grieving figure. She longs for sexual relationship and the companionship of a mate. If Ereshkigal is taken to be a metaphor for the Underworld and Pluto, then we witness Pluto's craving and desperation for life giving, procreative and therefore comforting, sexual fulfilment. This serves to remind us that relationships themselves can take us into the Underworld........ but so can lack of one! I quite often see clients whose life is a misery due to lack of relationship and therefore sexual fulfilment. If this misery is caused by Pluto's influence on them at that time, it is nice to be able to point out that Pluto's power is atomic, nuclear and definitely creative. We all have all the power we need at our fingertips to create a relationship.

The Meaning of Pluto in Astrology

The Discovery of Pluto the Planet

Events around the discovery of any planet tell us something of it's meaning, so we need to look at Pluto's.

Pluto was discovered in 1930 and was considered for many years to be the farthest planet from our Sun, (about 3.7 billion miles away) and certainly the smallest, at only 70% the size of our Moon.

But in the early 1930's science was also getting `smaller` with breakthroughs in sub-atomic science, the splitting of the atom, and the theoretical discovery of an unknown, invisible force or dark energy that made up two thirds of the Universe. As we know, in the early years of the 21st century this was finally proven to exist - just as Pluto hit the headlines again for being re-designated a `dwarf` planet.

The scientific breakthroughs of 1932 have been referred to as the "miracle year" of British physics[12], but the science was so hard to understand and explain, the journalists and public gave a yawn and turned to the sports page!

Plutonium was then manufactured and named after Pluto in 1941. The new scientific understanding led to an atom bomb being dropped on Japan. Destruction on this scale was too much to contemplate, and the human race turned away from atomic power.

The Traditional Meaning of Pluto in Astrology

In astrology we understand that Pluto is an agent for transformation and change. He represents evolution and the evolutionary force. I think that needs a little more explanation, so I looked up evolution in the dictionary: it means unrolling and unfolding; a gradual change over successive generations. It's also about expansion through enlargement and development. To evolve means to disclose, to progress and to mature. If you look back on that list, you will see there are some encouraging words there!

Pluto is an intelligent, ever present, ruling principle in the universal life force, which fulfills the cycle of evolution without restraint or sympathy. It is built into the very structure of life. If necessary, there will be a fight to the death, but it doesn't matter, because Pluto knows there will always be re-birth, a life after death, and ultimately life will always emerge. So although the destruction may be great, this should be seen in the light of the need for constant improvement - we have been told this is a maturing and progressive force.

The Pluto energy describes the circle or cycle of life, where there is life, death and re-birth in a never-ending cycle. It is a principle of generation and relentless growth and purging; an underlying code, in which the rules of nature are written. Pluto ends that which has outlived its usefulness, and sometimes in a remorseless way, but although the immense power might end the chapter and turn the page, Pluto also brings new life. This power was there in the creation, and is part of it, it never ceases to create.

According to astrologer Linda Goodman, the sacred number for this planet is zero, which represents power. She points out that we add a zero to numbers to increase their power, and the more zeros we add the more powerful something becomes.[13]

In ancient astrology, the circle represents the incomprehensible absolute unity and presence of all life – it's everything, so it's the dark and the light, for example. The source of all, it is present in all, it existed before our solar system, and it will exist after it has disappeared. This thing-that-can't-be-understood has no space or time limits.[14]

Pluto has a strong association with, or rules, the Zodiac sign of Scorpio. The Zodiac is simply the area around the Earth divided up into 12 portions. Let's say you are standing at the center of a cake; the Zodiac refers to the 12 wedges of cake that fan out around you. The part of sky called Scorpio is associated with Pluto and there are many similarities between the sign and the planet.

Scorpio also represents things that are buried and hidden, including deep knowledge, psychology and the secret power of the unconscious. Scorpio has associations with magnetic attraction, sexual activity and lust, which are all bound up with the important theme of procreation. Sexual union holds the potential to experience the intense currents of the great creative and generative force.[15] When two people are joined there is a potential for transformation on a soul level, as well as the potential to actually create new life. Sexual attraction and desire is a strange and mysterious thing that holds huge emotional energies, and Scorpionic people want to experience the crisis and euphoria of deep emotional exchange. These feelings create powerful urges and instinctual primal reactions, which can lead to triangles in love and toss victims into their own personal underworld of feelings and hell if it all goes wrong.

Pluto and the number 9

> "Plato regarded geometry as sacred, the Pythagoreans declared `All is number`, and the heading of the Egyptian Rhind Papyrus promises rules for enquiring into nature and for the knowing all that exists, every mystery, every secret."[16]

During the course of this project, curious co-incidences arose around the number 9. For instance:

A space mission was launched in 2006 to explore the Pluto family, and it will take 9 years to get there, arriving in 2015.

One of the recently discovered moons is called Hydra, a mythical beast with 9 heads, and the name was chosen with regard to Pluto's position as the 9th planet.[17]

A team of 9 astronomers found the two new moons, Nix and Hydra.[18]

In 1888, when only 8 planets were known to exist, an amazing lady called Helen Blavatsky wrote a huge book about science, religion and philosophy called The Secret Doctrine, in which she stated that the ancient Initiates of Vishnu knew of more than seven planets. "Parasara speaks of the chariots of the NINE planets which are attached by aerial cords to the Pole Star."[19]

According to the Egyptian Shabaka stone, Ptah gave birth to the 9 Neters or chief deities of Egypt.

A chap called Geoff Stray reported on a T.V. programme in 2009 that nine was also important to the Mayans, who predicted that 2012 would see the return of the Nine....
...........the rest of the stone tablet had been destroyed so I'll just have to leave that dangling......

What does all that mean?

According to the astrologer, Linda Goodman[20] 9 represents `material life` and the beginning and end of life on the material plane of existence. She goes on to say that multiplying cannot destroy 9 and this is true of no other number.

For instance:	2 x 9 = 18 then add 1 + 8 and you get 9
	3 x 9 = 27 then add 2 + 7 and you get 9
	14 x 9 = 126 add 1 + 2 + 6 and you get.....9!

This gets more interesting when she describes how 9 gives life back to each of the single numbers.

For instance:	9 plus **1** = 10 1 plus 0 = **1** again
	9 plus **2** = 11 1 plus 1 = **2** again
	9 plus 4 = 13 1 plus 3 = **4** again

There are more examples of these, but her point is that 9 is the king of numbers, the sacred number of eternity, and the entire edifice upon which human life on this planet is based. This is comforting since it cannot be destroyed!

In astrology 9 represents conflict, strife and the ability to penetrate and this meaning is compatible with the effect the planet tends to have on people. The actual planet of Pluto has the number of 0, but I think the additional message of `9` energy, which seems important at this time, gives us another layer of meaning to contemplate. Let's look again at Linda Goodman's words. The number 9 represents material life, and the beginning and ending of this material life. Material life is all the `matter`. All the planets and stars, our Earth, the whole human race and everything that we can see or feel.

In his book, Serpent in the Sky, West says nine is extremely complex. Nine emanates from the absolute divine; it is "interpenetrating, interacting and interlocked." So it's like the fabric or matrix of interwoven existence. In recent years science has become obsessed with finding the origins of life. Billions of pounds are being spent on sophisticated instruments dedicated to a single focus – what's the theory of everything? The single equation that will give a provable, undeniable paper explanation. The two frontiers of exploration, space/cosmos/huge and sub-atomic/quantum/tiny, are coming together in an effort to get THE answer. The emphasis on the number 9 surrounding Pluto is a reflection of this.

The Serpent as a Symbol of Healing and Magic

There are two symbols in common use by the medical profession. One is a serpent winding up a staff, and the other is……the caduceus, TWO serpents winding up a staff. Organisations such as the World Health Organisation and the Paramedics of the National Health Service proudly display these symbols.

> "The serpent upon the staff was quiet universally the symbol among the ancients of the medical art. The serpent signified the principle of occult life, and the staff or rod was the symbol of magic power."[21]

Astrology has always understood Scorpio's rulership over healing and the healing arts, and this won't cause a problem to most people. But Scorpio also rules magic and the occult, and this is something that the medical profession certainly doesn't want to be associated! Certain medical associations in America are now trying to disassociate from the caduceus, the two serpent version, because it is associated with Hermes, the Greek God who is associated with the Hermetic texts and secret doctrine.[22] (This, they say, is paganism, witchcraft and magic.....and astrology. My my, how awful.) The Hermetic texts were copied from even earlier documents that may have been written in Egypt between 3,000-1,000B.C.E. and contained vastly superior medical and philosophical knowledge. This knowledge was destroyed as civilisation headed towards the arrival of the one-god religious dynasties after 01.A.D. Hermes was watered down to become a winged messenger god who could pass between the Underworld and the Upperworld and often escorted souls. He can be seen in the illustration at the beginning of this chapter. Even in this watered down version, he still sends a clear message that wisdom and knowledge will help us mortals in our dealings with the Underworld.

In ancient Egypt magic and healing were taken as the same thing. They called on the supernatural by chanting invocations whilst they were treating the patient. This would have invoked the secret power of the un-conscious, which is what is also invoked during the healing ceremony of Reiki, this is often called the Placebo effect by medical science.

I took this quote from a book on the website of Professor Ralph Abraham (Princeton, Berkeley and California Universities):

> "With these spells, evolved over centuries, one might....communicate with the gods, command subtle energies, acquire wealth, health......The most powerful allies were the gods and goddesses of the underworld: Erishkegal, Persephone Hekate and the like. We are left with the impression that magic is a human creation which exists on a level above religion. While religions come and go, magic is eternal."[23]

Whilst Scorpio is indeed associated with the mastery of healing, there are 2 sides to the coin, and I will just remind you about the myth involving Asclepius, who is the Greek god of medicine that the medical profession these days *do* want to be associated with. (His is the rod with the single serpent on it.) Asclepius was curing so many people and even bringing so many back from the dead, that Pluto feared that he would have no more souls left in the Underworld, so he asked Zeus to kill Asclepius. He was duly wiped out with a thunderbolt, and became a constellation in the sky. The interesting point here is that Pluto *must* maintain the amount of souls on the journey. This process must continue above all efforts to preserve life here on earth. So the medical profession had better watch out...because if they keep too many alive they'll all get the old thunderbolt treatment! What Pluto gives, Pluto can also remove.

Out of interest, a doctor today swears a Hippocratic oath as he qualifies. Hippocrates was an astrologer and his medicine was based on the movement of the heavens. He would not advocate surgery when the Moon was in the zodiac sign connected to that part of the body, and he warned of the rising of certain stars such as Sirius.

The Difference Between Dark Feminine and Dark Masculine

If Tiamat is an expression of the extreme dark face of feminine, then what is the extreme dark face of masculine? To answer this question we have to first recognise that the dark face of feminine is about extreme ***feelings***. So the opposite, dark masculine, has to be about an extreme lack of feelings, and this then is psychopathy. A human being is psychopathic when s/he is devoid of feelings. An extreme example of this can be found in the fascist behaviour of Nazi Germany, where they took a dream of perfection and idealism into the extremes of feelinglessness and it became destructive. In this way `destroying` occurs in both dark feminine and dark masculine. Dark masculine is the `hero` on the hero's journey taken to extreme, the zealous militant with ideals of perfectionism and a Utopian vision.

Imagine for a moment a circle. (As the astrolological number for Pluto is O, then this seems quite fitting.) This circle is the circle of life, and everything in life goes round in a continuous circle. Now imagine 2 `poles` like the North and South poles of our planet. Masculine and feminine are polar opposites, with one at the top and one at the bottom, but they blend into each other at the Equator, where things could be considered balanced. In this way, masculine emerges out of feminine and then feminine emerges out of masculine. As with the chicken and the egg, I don't think we'll ever know which came first! Being at the extreme `pole` of either is ugly, but I have to admit that of the 2 options feminine can seem the most attractive when we ask the question "Who wants to be cured of feelings and desire?"

I see Pluto as representing feminine energy despite the fact that the name Pluto comes from a male Greek god. I can sense and feel this as an astrologer. So often both clients and my own experiences speak eloquently of the rage, fury and wrath that comes with Pluto experiences. There are often power struggles and intense jealousies, with the birth of babies or marriage quiet common during the times that we are personally receiving energy from Pluto. (The birth of babies can cause power struggles and intense jealousies between siblings and spouses, whilst marriages can have a similar impact on pre-existing children or ex-partners.) Feelings of protective primal savagery can tap us on the shoulder when we are creating something that stirs us deeply and we want to protect it at all costs.

What We Can Expect to Gain, Change and Develop in the 21st Century?

We Shall Find Parallel Universes - the Underworld and Heaven of Mythology

According to top physicist Professor Max Tegmark "The key question is not whether parallel universes exist...... but how many levels there are."[24]

Because Pluto represents hidden realms and dimensions we can expect `quantum leaps` of discovery in this area. We could never have imagined in the 1980's that scientists would be using words like `ether`, and discussing particles that pop in and out of our dimension. The spiritual and mythological claims that dark, unseen dimensions existed was scoffed at and ridiculed by many mainstream academics. Now we get such eminent scientists as Brian Greene telling us that

> "The entire Universe is this gigantic loaf with many other slices, potentially. So our Universe could be one slice, and a different parallel Universe could be living on a different slice."[25]

It is my intention in this book to establish the probability that these parallel universes include the Underworld or Duat of the very ancient civilizations, and also the Heaven of more recent religions. I don't assign the Christian image of Hell there since I think it more likely the 4% and this world might be the hell bit, since it is such hard work and contains so much atrocity.

Scientific exploration is proceeding at a breath taking pace and the books are out of date before they are even printed these days. Such is this pace that we will no doubt have as much inter-dimensional experience as we can manage to understand before the first decade of the 21st century has ended. As this unfolds, there is an amazing similarity between the descriptions and words of the spiritual texts left us from many thousands of years ago, and the scientific discoveries of now. The two seem to be converging into a common knowledge, which is interesting since neither party wants to be identified with a view that they had previously considered un-enlightened. It is, however, very gratifying for those of us who have upheld spiritual knowledge for all these years, in spite of a sniffy and dismissive scientific establishment.

The Changes to Pluto Coincide with the Development of the Large Hadron Collider

As I write this, we are witnessing the launch of the most ambitious experiment that science has ever taken on. It is a project involving the largest machine ever built, called the Large Hadron Collider (L.H.C.), and it's mission is to discover tiny, invisible particles of energy that will inform us of parallel universes and other dimensions. The whole project was synchronous with Pluto from the beginning, and it is interesting to look at what has been happening to Pluto the planet, with reference to the progress of the project.

There is a little about the L.H.C. in the chapter on Cool Science, but more should be said about it now.

The scientists involved in the project are trying to find the answer to the question - what is matter made of? We know that it is made of cells, and cells are made of molecules, and molecules are made of atoms and atoms are made of smaller bits called particles. But when they look into these particles they find lots of spinning energy and what looks like empty space. *Something* has to provide atoms with weight/mass/substance, but where is it? The theory is that there are **invisible** undetectable `dark` particles and dark matter, which if accounted for, will explain how an atom is rigid. These dark particles probably exist in a 4th dimension that intertwines with ours and the L.H.C. has been constructed to find this other dimension.

To find the dark particles, they send beams of energy with particles of `real` matter in it whizzing round inside an underground circular tube at the speed of light. Then they send another one in the opposite direction. Periodically these smash into each other, and large detectors measure the invisible energy that is released. Measuring this released energy tells them about the dark particles in the other dimension.

One of the most obvious symbols of relationship between Pluto and the L.H.C. is the shape. It is a 27 km long tunnel formed into a circle, and the beams it produces go around and around inside it. Not only is this the shape of the number zero, which is the sacred number of Pluto; the circle is also the symbol of the cycle of life. Another obvious synchronicity is the L.H.C.'s physical position, buried deep within the bowels of the Earth – a real under-world!

In 1995 Pluto moved into the 9th Zodiac sign, Sagittarius, which is the part of the sky most associated with the search for the TRUTH and the spiritual meaning of life. When Pluto moves through any Zodiac sign it is expected that world wide events will focus on the meanings of that sign, and certainly the quest and journey that sub atomic physics has been on has been very descriptive of Sagittarius, with huge leaps into wild, un-bridled theories and breakthroughs. The European consortium that built the L.H.C. reported that their energy capacity for sub-atomic research doubled in the year that Pluto moved into Sagittarius "opening up important new discovery domains."[26] Sagittarius describes higher spiritual learning, and the seeking of the vision of the Divine. During the years that Pluto was in this sign, from 1995 to 2008, the L.H.C. was being built with a vision of the possibility of finding the origins of life.

In 2006 things began to get really exciting. Pluto lined up between the Earth and the center of our galaxy, which is in the last few degrees of Sagittarius. This point is known in astrology to be immensely powerful, there is a large black hole there in reality, and it had the effect of plugging Pluto energy into the national grid. All the digging and building work at the L.H.C. ended and they actually started installing and operating the very high voltage, massive machines that would enable their sub-atomic research. For the next 2 years, from 2006 to 2008, all sorts of milestones and early experimental achievements were completed, and the project really came together. Then, as Pluto stood for the last few days close to the galactic center, the first beams of energy were officially sent all the way around the ring at the L.H.C. for the first time and the machine started up. The timing of the 2 events was incredibly co-incidental, and as if to confirm the astrological importance, our Moon also joined Pluto there for a few hours. Her quiet and reflective light providing the calm before the storm of worldwide media attention the next day.

The press coverage before the inauguration invoked the usual responses that Pluto tends to have on people. Some embraced the future possibilities with excitement, some ignored it for now (but the changes will come anyway), and others become fearful of catastrophe and tried to prevent it all happening with legal challenges. It was interesting to see that the P.R. people in charge began selling the project with the line that they were attempting to re-create the moment after the Big Bang. This might be true enough, but it glossed over the fact that they were looking for evidence of energy reappearing and disappearing into other dimensions. The `other dimensions` talk had frightened the press and public into thinking that the Earth was going to disappear into a black hole, so this aspect of the research became underplayed.

The Zodiac sign after Sagittarius is Capricorn, and Pluto moved fully into this earth sign in November 2008. Since the L.H.C. intends to smash ions of lead together, it seems amazing that his should happen just at the time that Pluto moves into the Zodiac sign most associated with lead and dense matter. Capricorn is the highest initiation of matter and the earth element, and is ruled by Saturn, the planet that ruled the outer limits of our known world for thousands of years. Those `outer limits` are a frontier that will be well and truly smashed in the 21st century!

The Development and Acceptance of Atomic Energy

The term `nuclear` comes from the `nucleus` of an atom, and in an atom there is a force so strong it can be turned into a bomb that will destroy a whole city. There are understandable deeply rooted public concerns about nuclear power. Many of those alive today can remember the fear invoked by the use of the atom bomb and it's constant threatened use during the 20th century. Add to that the accidents caused by the bad management of atomic processes, such as the accident at Chernobyl, and it absolutely understandable why the public are so against it. Concerns range from the disposal of the radioactive waste product, to the easy production of nuclear weapons if countries engage in it. But nuclear bombs were built before anybody thought of using it to produce electricity. When they built and used the bombs in 1945 there were no nuclear reactors in existence. Proof that countries can build bombs without nuclear power stations.

The nuclear industry is now keen to point out that if nuclear power stations are properly managed then they are an environmentally safe, pollution free source of electricity. According to the chairman of the International Atomic Energy Agency in 2004,

> "in contrast with the 25 *billion* tonnes of carbon waste released directly into the atmosphere every year from fossil fuels, the amount of nuclear waste seems relatively small."[27]

I suspect that governments will be backed into a corner over their current disinclination towards building any more nuclear power stations, because the fossil fuel option will not be available for much longer. New options should open up with regard to nuclear power however, with maybe a whole new way of using the latent power trapped in the nucleus of an atom. Invisible forces of nature may become known and available to us.

Can we Change Our Perception of Evil and the Devil?

Unfortunately, a few Dennis Wheatley films, and 2,000 years of being told that terror and damnation awaits us in an Underworld of burning hell fires and purgatory have left us with huge fear and trembling. (The burning hell fire image comes from the volcanoes of Italy where the Catholic faith is centred.) This fear stops us from feeling comfortable about an enthusiastic investigation into the contents of Pluto's box. The words Hades and death have become synonymous with evil. But the Underworld is not filled with evil or horned goblins with toasting forks, and I think our society will now finally emerge from the teachings and shadow of the Middle Ages. There *is* another dimension or parallel universe, and science has now proven that, but it supports our Universe and we should not fear it.

Really evil acts of a barbaric and psychotic nature do happen, this is undeniable, but these happen because of mental illness, fear, ignorance, or the primordial, brutal, animalistic instincts that remain hard wired into our human nature. This instinct is a relic of some savage and prehistoric past, when we had to go out and club the beast and drag it back by it's hair. It was necessary then to take a knife to the throat of a living animal, but obviously the evolution of Western society has removed the need for most individuals to engage in this now. However, the ability to kill still remains deeply embedded in our genetic inheritance, should we ever find ourselves in need of it again in future centuries. Having that potential on the hard drive of human D.N.A. is protective of the human race should the flood or the apocalypse ever happen again. It means that any survivors will have the potential to kill and eat, and survival of the fittest will ensure that strong and robust parents give birth to strong and robust children. The human race will survive and flourish again. This is the underlying code of universal natural law, which will maintain the procreation and survival of the human race at any cost to single human life. This is what Pluto really represents. Pluto doesn't have to be barbaric. It can be, but this energy is not naturally destructive for the sake of it. It has a purpose.

The image of Pluto, Hades and the Underworld is one that we are trying to avoid in today's technically advanced society. A lot of scientists scoff at the idea of god or the devil and believe that they can confine Pluto it to a petri-dish, remove the undesirable and control the outcome.

The more spiritually inclined of us flinch from `dark` issues like Satan and death, preferring to talk pink, fluffy angels all the time. It is hard to accept and deal with the destructive, dark and painful forces that threaten disintegration of cherished ideals. But by refusing to know the dark side, we move away form the possibility of a deep and real understanding of it. Perhaps we are throwing the baby out with the bath water. We actually need to gain a *deeper* knowledge and mastery of the unconscious, and the fundamental forces of our life here on earth. As far as astrology and science is concerned, we all have a dark side....each and every one of us, but it's how much fear, ignorance and impotence controls us that regulates it's effects on our lives. The more we understand something, the greater our intelligence and the more we are empowered. We have more options or choice, because we can consider more. Modern psychology believes that anything we fear and push into our unconscious simply gathers more energy and re-routes. It may then pop up as energy that we constellate or magnetise into our lives. It may appear as if it is entirely another person's doing, but it will appear. And then we are *really* ill equipped to deal with it.

One of the things that Scorpio is traditionally known for is the `occult`. This word always conjures up thoughts of witchcraft and evil, but let's look at what it means. The definition of occult in my dictionary is:

> "Involving mystical or supernatural phenomena or powers. Beyond ordinary human understanding. Secret or mysterious."

Supernatural is "something that cannot be explained by science." So the word occult by itself is not that scary. Satan is a fear in our minds

The changing of Pluto's official status from planet to binary planetoid system has symbolized an immense and imminent universal change. Perhaps now we can seek to understand the emerging power, with all the taboo issues and fearfulness that this brings. We might want to understand for our spiritual peace of mind, but also so we can work with this omnipresent cosmic force, perhaps see the beauty, elegance and magnificence; and at least become over-awed and respectful of the immense power it wields. It is likely that healing and growth can be found through the mastery and understanding that a thorough examination of the Underworld can bring.

Let's look at the meaning of the word `Pluto`. The word comes from the Greek word `plouton` meaning wealth. Another definition is `rich`. I truly believe there are riches that can be gained from Pluto's world, if we are willing to accept a rough ride with trust and faith in a higher divine power.

Understanding the Meaning of Life Can Change Our Attitude to Death and the Afterlife

I have written on how we might change our attitude to death in the chapter on Ceres, but I would like to just touch on the whole subject here. Since fear is usually brought about by not knowing, the `knowing` that we are likely to get in the near future should alleviate the terrible fear that death invokes in us. Loss will still occur as loved ones pass on into the 96% and mourning for the loss of the loved one is an essential part of being human, but a much deeper understanding of *why* it has to happen is now available. Knowing the Meaning of Life, and the part our soul plays in it, answers questions that our curiosity has yearned for centuries. At last, that information is here for us gain.

Very basically, there is a Multiverse of many universes. Life as we know it occurs in just one universe, and this is everything we know- all the planets, stars and Earth. This is just 4% of the Multiverse. The dark or missing 96% is the rest of the Multiverse and it includes an Underworld that our soul goes to when we die. Our deceased soul empties out it's life experiences and wisdom into the collective ocean or great soup of Collective Soul. And our soul's contribution improves the overall wisdom and experience of this Collective Soul. Our soul is then re-cycled on into the next appropriate `life` cycle. This might be back to the Earthly plane in the 4%, or on to higher transcendence.

The human race has to survive at all costs, because this is the Multiverse's only solid expression of the energy and intelligence that exists in the chaos and timelessness of the 96%.

If you just followed that, you may not need the rest of this book!

A lot of that is not new; we have been told it by our ancient texts. What is new is that the Underworld is one of these other parallel universes or dimensions.

Miraculous Healing Potential, Reiki and Kundalini.

Numerous web sites equate the power of the serpent with kundalini reiki. In `Myths and Gods of India` we are told that Siva carries a snake around his neck and phallus, and:

> "…the main meaning attached to the serpent is to represent the basic dormant energy, akin to the sexual power, which is coiled at the base of the spinal cord, and supports attempts to conquer higher worlds during inward journeys. This energy, source of all spiritual conquests, is called Kundalini, the coiled serpent power."[28]

According to a professional American medical website:

> "An occult description of the (staff with 2 snakes winding up it) is that the serpents may represent positive and negative kundalini as it moves through the chakras and around the spine (the staff) to the head where it communicates with mind….."[29]

Kundalini contains the potential for spiritual transformation and is often activated by big life events such as a near death experience or the birth of a child. Whilst this might sound frightening, it should be stressed that kundalini is the Hindu word for sacred, transformative, awakening energy, and surely this is sort by anyone who seeks spiritual enlightenment. It seems intense and powerful life events have the potential to take us into higher states of consciousness, and this is whether they are willingly sort in a peaceful meditative way, or whether they come with tragedy and loss. Either way, Pluto's generative abilities are being accessed in these periods of immense change and transformation, and that's an awful lot of nuclear power to have at your disposal! It is during these periods that the `wealth` of Pluto is available on a soul level.

`Myths of India` infers that the same kundalini energy is available in a universal, macro form, when it gives birth to the Universe, and in a personal, micro form, when it can lead to awakening and liberation. As astrology is telling us that Pluto is going to become much more accessible and understandable in the forthcoming years, then the implication is that we will all be able to access much greater personal awakening, including that of our individual latent healing potential. Medical science is already recording the effects of this.

The placebo effect is the name given to a positive result achieved in a patient who has been administered false medication (a sugar pill) in a medical trial. New Scientist reported in late 2008: ".....the placebo effect appears to be growing stronger in clinical trials, causing problems for drug companies attempting to prove their products are better than placebo."[30]

This is evidence of the growing power of the human consciousness to access the power of the deep realms, and bring about miraculous healing. This is exceptionally good news for Reiki, which taps into deep personal realms and deep universal realms for it's Pluto-nic energy.

Just one more thing whilst we are on the subject of healing. Take a moment to think about what is required to get rid of a pimple or boil. It needs to be destroyed and the poison routed out before the healing can begin. Pluto is the energy that will bring about the end of something....... without it.......... the boil would just go on forever!

Transformation, Evolution and `Wealth` on a Soul Level

When a client comes to me asking for information about when they can get out of the bad marriage/inappropriate job/wrong home, the first thing I look for are the dates when Pluto will be influencing them, and those are the dates they get! With the right advice they can channel, bend and transpose the incoming energy at that time to get the changes they dream of, although they must be prepared to accept a lot of change, some of which may include loss. In astrology, Pluto represents a powerful energy that will challenge or assist our journey to higher consciousness, although it has always been the most feared.

However, we are told in the myths of Persephone and Inanna, that we ***will*** come out of the Underworld again, and we will have gained much wealth and riches during our time in the depths. It is now time to accept transformation, evolution and wealth would good grace!

Chapter 5

Illustration 7. *A mortal getting into Charon's boat, watched over by Hermes.*

CHARON, GUIDE TO PLUTO AND THE INVISIBLE REALMS

Charon, A Partner For Pluto

Now here's a planet you won't have heard of! For many years Pluto was the last and furthest planet from the Sun – 3,700,000,000 miles away to be precise-ish. So far away that we have never sent a spacecraft or probe there, and all we have is some hazy pictures of a distant blob of light. More recently, our space instruments and telescopes have become much more sophisticated and we have started to learn a lot more. Surprisingly, we found out that Pluto has a partner planet joined to him called Charon, *and* there are an additional 2 moons around them. That's four different things where we used to think that was one. The point I'm making here, is the very close relationship between our discoveries about Pluto and the discoveries that are being made of the particles in an atom. An atom has been found to have more bits and planet Pluto's neighbourhood in space has loads more than was previously thought. Discoveries in one area of our world are always synchronous with discoveries in another.

How Charon Was Discovered

Back in 1978 a U.S. Navy astronomer was doing some precise observations of Pluto, which had been scheduled because Pluto had moved a bit closer to the Sun than he normally is. In fact Pluto had even moved *inside* the orbit of next planet, which he does for only 20 years of his 248 year cycle around the Sun. The astronomer, James Christy, noticed that some of the photographs of the distant blob of light (Pluto) appeared to show a bulge of light at the side of the planet, and after much checking it was officially announced to the world that this bulge of light was actually a separate `moon` and it was given the name Charon. Soon after discovery, Charon and Pluto obligingly posed for photographs by getting into a position that made it easy for astronomers to see and measure them. The timing was amazing because the pair wouldn't be in this easily photographable position again for centuries.[1]

The discoverer named Charon after the ferryman of Greek mythology, who takes the souls of the dead across a river into the Underworld. He asked that Charon be pronounced *Shar-on,* after his wife Charlene.[2]

Because astronomers can only estimate the size of such far off things by measuring the amount of light they reflect, the discovery of Charon had the immediate impact of changing all previous perceptions about the size of Pluto. Now that the light given off it had to be divided by two, it meant that that Pluto was not as bright, and therefore not as big. As our perception of Pluto was divided into smaller bits, so was our perception of the atom.

Pluto and Charon are locked into each other in the same way that the two ends of a dumbbell are attached to each other. It's as if an invisible shaft holds them together. They are so close, the centre of gravity for each planet is not within itself, but in the space in between the two planets, and their two faces are permanently frozen together.

As the 21st century dawned a team of astronomers were busy setting up equipment for the survey that would discover what was in the Kuiper Belt, which is the region around Pluto and Charon. The new planets they discovered are in the chapters following this, but we just need to look at one thing about that survey that had big impact on Pluto and Charon.

Because the survey discovered more planets after Pluto-Charon and they didn't want to keep re-writing all the schoolbooks, they had to think up a different definition for the term `planet`. The new definition meant that Charon qualified for the new term `dwarf planet` and in 2006 this was announced. A big step up for Charon.[3] However, that same announcement changed Pluto from a planet to a dwarf planet – so a step down for Pluto! This made them a very unusual double dwarf planet or `binary` planet, and there is a lot of spiritual meaning that can be inferred by this, as we shall see later.

Charon Is Struggling To Be Accepted

Even though all the above happened as stated, there has since been a problem and Charon's designation as dwarf planet has not found acceptance in some astronomers. The I.A.U. started to dither about his new title and at the time of writing in 2009, it is difficult to find mention of Charon anywhere on the internet. The other dwarf planets are heavily promoted by their extrovert and enthusiastic discoverer, Mike Brown, but it seems that Charon's half-life in the shadow of Pluto is going to be hard to shake off. However, there will be more interest in future years when a space probe arrives at Pluto-Charon in 2015. This mission was launched by N.A.S.A. in January 2006 and is called New Horizons.

It is interesting that the L.H.C. project has also stalled because of technical breakdown and one is left wondering if the two things are synchronous.

The Mythological World of Ancient Greece and How This Might Represent The Multiverse

On 15th May 2005, 2 little moons were discovered around Pluto-Charon, and they are called Nix and Hydra, so the whole Pluto-Charon family have been given mythological names from the ancient Greek Underworld. Before we go on to look at what that might mean, it is useful to see how the ancient Greeks viewed the Multiverse.

They had three `realms` in their myths; the Upperworld of mortal humans, the Underworld - where the souls or shades of the dead mortals go and Olympus.

Olympus is the home of the king of the gods, Zeus and his family. It was supposedly high up a mountain and protected by a gate shrouded in clouds.[4] Other god/desses might have their abode in the earth or the water of the Upperworld, but they could go to Olympus to join or feast with the royal god/desses that resided there.

The `Heavens`, were mentioned as a starry celestial backdrop to Olympus, a stage which they could play things out on if they wished.[5] A god could be banished to the stars where he would become a constellation, or a pattern of stars, but once thrown there, that's what he became, and that's where he stayed. Whilst Olympus itself was actually a separate place, the god/desses mostly intermingled with the mortals on Earth, (Upperworld) and their lives were intertwined with ours, although often invisibly so. The Underworld could be reached from the Upperworld or from the Heavens.

Are these two mythological places metaphors for the dimensions that the scientists will now discover? We will find dimensions that exists along side and intertwined with ours. Maybe we can interpret one as the Underworld, a repository or great lake of soul energy in which our souls are re-cycled, and maybe there is another which is like Olympus, full of spirit, energy, and represents the God-ness and the spiritual element of fire.

The Myths of Charon, Nix and Hydra From the Underworld

Charon is the ancient Greek name given to a mythical ferryman who takes the souls of the dead across a river into the Underworld. Bulfinch's Mythology says:

> "They then came to black river, where they found the ferryman, Charon, old and squalid, but strong and vigorous, who was receiving passengers of all kinds into his boat…..they stood pressing for a passage and longing to touch the opposite shore. But the stern ferryman took in only such as he chose, driving the rest back…….Those who are taken on board the bark are the souls of those who have received due burial rites; the host of others who have remained unburied are not permitted to pass the flood, but wander a hundred years…until at last they are taken over (the river)."[6]

The story then relates how two living people were allowed to get into the bark (boat) and travel across the river because they had a golden branch with them, a symbol that Charon recognizes. Actually I found at least four mythical instances of the living going into the Underworld and getting out again, so clearly it *can* be done, although all the myths initially give it a `land-of-no-return` image. Those that do praise the process for the riches it gives. Elsewhere we learn that Charon expects coins in payment for his ferrying of the souls of the dead. In the past, a coin used to be placed under the tongue of the deceased. (Better get yourself some coins then!)[7] Another snippet tells us that as the souls stand on the bank waiting to be ferried by Charon, they look like birds as they gather together to seek warmer climes at the first chill of winter, or leaves waiting to fall from the branches in winter.[8]

In myth, Charon comes out of a wonderfully gloomy family, which reinforces the dark underworld theme of the whole clan. His mother is a Greek deity called Nyx, and a derivation of this name was given to one of the two Pluto-Charon moons found in 2006, so we kill two birds with one stone if we look at the origins surrounding that mythological family. In a nutshell, the whole clan is about the creation. Charon's grandmother is Chaos, the original nothingness, which was there before there was anything. Therefore she is the quantum energy of pre-existence, what was there in the beginning, before the Big Bang.

Chaos created Erebos, who is called primordial darkness or the darkness of the Underworld,[9] and his sister, Nyx, who is the goddess of the night or the darkness of the Earth. They gave birth to many children, a particularly gloomy lot with names that imply Doom of Death, Fate of Death, Sleep, Dreams, Criticism, Deceit, Sex, Old Age, and Strife, to name but a few. However, she also gave birth to Ether, Day and Air, symbolising the equal power of both light and dark, and in one myth it says that she also gave birth to Eros, god of desire, who was known for shooting his arrow at people to make them fall in lust.

Although Nyx was rarely mentioned in Greek myth, her power was emphasised when it was said that Zeus backed away from her in one encounter - an unimaginable event, considering he was the King of the Gods with a temper and ego to match. She was sometimes represented as a veil of dark mist, drawn forth from the Underworld, which blotted out the light.[10]

The last myth we have to look at is that of Hydra, the other moon that was discovered in 2006. Hydra was a serpent or water snake of Greek mythology that lived in a marsh near the mouth of the Underworld and had nine heads. If a head was severed, 2 grew back in it's place. Hercules was sent to kill this monster as the second of his 12 labours. He used fire to cauterise the wound of each head as it fell off so that none could grow in it's place. This might represent one of those problems that seems to get bigger as you attack it, and so might need a constantly positive belief in the power of spirit. After killing the beast, Hercules dipped 2 arrows in the poisonous blood and these arrows caused him to harm 2 friends, and eventually brought about his own death. Perhaps the moral of the story is after the fight and the victory, don't take any of the venom with you……..It will have dire consequences on your friendships if you do!

The Spiritual Meaning of Charon

The Importance of the Ferryman in Significant Ancient Texts.

The most ancient texts of the Egyptians and the Mesopotamians (the first master race who lived in Iraq) also have ferrymen. The Pyramid Texts of ancient Egypt, written around 3,000B.C.E. say: *"Hdhd,* the ferryman of the Winding Watercourse, comes...."[11] Hundreds of miles away and maybe a thousand years later, the Mesopotamian myth called the `Epic of Gilgamesh`, written in approx. 2,000 B.C.E. advises us that a boatman crosses the waters of Death...[12]

So the idea of a ferryman rowing over an expanse of water during an incredible journey of discovery has remained for at least 5,000 years. Not much else has been that durable. It's a simple idea, but it begs the question - Why has Charon suddenly become important to astrology and why is that important to the human race now? Why do we need a Ferryman again?

A Symbol of the Beginning of an Immense and Epic Journey of Discovery for the Human Race.

If you've made it this far, dear reader, then you are about to find out why I am making such a big (but hopefully not that boring) deal out of this whole Charon thing!

The ancients knew that immense journeys of discovery required a spiritual guide. We are being told that we are going on a journey of discovery, and something or someone is going to guide us through this potentially difficult passage. Charon the Ferryman was not just the tour guide, he decided who got on the bus and whether or not they were spiritually prepared enough to board.

As a planet, he managed to hide from us his very existence until such time as we were ready. It's as if the planet (or godness) is saying "ok, you have created the `tech-knowledgy` to discover my presence; this technology will now take you on a big journey, and I am here as your stern guide and overseer."

Ok, so what's the journey?

Well, it could be the discovery of the other dimensions. If we use our solar system as an analogy, then the Pluto-Charon family represents the Underworld, and that is within the larger Kuiper Belt, which in general represents the other dimensions of the Multiverse. (Get another glass of wine perhaps?) Pluto-Charon is like a sentry or gateway into the Kuiper Belt. All right, if we are going to split hairs, there *are* other ways into the Kuiper Belt - we could point a rocket in any direction outwards from the Earth and it will get their eventually, since the Kuiper Belt surrounds us. But Pluto-Charon was the first known bit of it, and that's the bit we are sending a space probe to first. So the metaphor is saying we have to enter the Underworld, or cross over from our dimension into the Underworld in order to access the dimensions from whence we came. If you remember back to the Ceres chapter, we were told this by the ancient Egyptians. Charon is the ferryman who stands at the entry point or gateway, just as he does in the myth. He will allow us passage if we are properly prepared, but not before.

Another journey might be our journey into the discovery of our origins, which is similar of course. The Greek myth of creation actually says that in the beginning was Chaos and this gave birth to Night, Darkness and Day etc. and the human race is currently discovering the science of that creation, about our formation out of pure energy and chaotic quantum-ruled atoms. How we emerged from the energy of pre-existence into the world of matter and form that we know. The `fall` of Man, or the Big Bang, is when our Universe fell out of the quantum chaos of the primordial soup into the order of the Upperworld.[13]

What Does Duality Mean?

NASA says, "Pluto has a dual identity."[14] The dwarf planets, Pluto and Charon, are locked into each other with their two faces joined together, as if with an invisible shaft joins them. Like a giant dumbbell spinning in space. We are being asked to understand that the most powerful force in astrology is now two, not one. That Pluto has another face, and that there is another side to this energy.

Duality was highly prized by the Ancient Egyptians, and they used the serpent to symbolize it. So what is duality about and why is it important?

Well, to start with, the dictionary says that duality means having two parts, functions or aspects. This might be useful because we don't know what anything is, until we can see the difference. If we live in perpetual light, how do we know what dark is? Only after it has turned dark do we notice the difference and ask, "What was it that has gone missing? What is this that I am in now?"

The ability or faculty to think about the meaning of opposites gives a framework in which we can use free will to organise and balance our lives. If you can see that this is white, but you want to be more black, you can use absolute black and absolute white as your outer markers, and aim for dark or light grey, depending on your choice. Having duality, or two parts, functions or aspects, to choose from or measure by, is giving us choice.

Then we discriminate, we think this way, then that way. We analyse and develop intelligence and intuition along the way. We create opportunity and then we destroy it when it is past it's sell by date. We use the energy of Pluto to build and dismantle.

And why is that important?

There are millions of souls on a spiral journey of evolution, and they must all contribute to a rising of the universal collective `mind` into higher consciousness. Our separate bits of knowledge and understanding are gathered together to move the whole of life onto higher planes of awareness. Things like choices and dual importance create the friction and tension that make us work at balance and greater awareness and wisdom. We improve and refine ourselves as we work to explore the different options that are in front of us.

The coins we have to pay the Ferryman in the myth are the pearls of wisdom we have gained in our lives. Remember in the myth if we don't have enough coins to pay the ferryman, we are left to wander the banks of the River for a time? The more often we grow and evolve through the crisis and change which Pluto's world invokes, the more often we benefit by having the right amount of coins. In Greek, the word Pluto comes from the word plouton, which means wealth or rich.

For 40 years very little was discovered in our Solar System. Then we went through a period of accelerated discovery from 2003 until 2006 ish. It means the human race is leaping forward in spiritual understanding too. However, the ferryman clearly thinks the time has come for us to understand the Underworld, which we are told holds wealth and richness. The payoffs will be a source of atomic power that is safe for our planet, scientific understanding of other dimensions and other Universes in the Multiverse and an understanding of our creation.

The Ferryman has come to show us the real truth about the Underworld.........Charon is guiding us on a whole new journey.

Illustration 8. *An image of Makemake carved on a rock on Easter Island*

MAKEMAKE, THE GREAT SEA SPIRIT OF EASTER ISLAND

Our journey now leaves the ancient Greek Underworld and we travel many thousands of Earth miles to the Pacific Ocean. Here we visit two Polynesian islands. The first, Easter Island the home of Makemake, and then Hawaii, the home of Haumea.

Astrology reflects what is happening in our collective, and so astrology needed some new symbols to represent the issues of the new millennium. We needed to have new energies or god/desses that will walk with us during the frantic change of the 21st century. It was surprising when these came from way outside the normal sources, and it will take us some time to understand what they mean in depth, but this chapter is a start. Well, quite a big start actually! It is easily the biggest chapter in this book, but this is no reflection of Makemake's strength or prominence over the rest of the dwarf planets, since there are others that feel stronger. It is simply that there is so much that we weren't aware of before. Prepare for an amazing story if you have not yet heard the history of Easter Island.

Makemake, the Dwarf Planet

Possibly one of the biggest difficulties this dwarf planet may have in gaining public affection is the fact that his name is confusing to pronounce. If you can say something without feeling dumb or disrespectful it has more endearing qualities! However, I suspect when you have finished this chapter you will look again at that name, and this time you will see it differently.

Makemake is one of four newly discovered dwarf planets in the far distant outskirts of our solar system, the region called the Kuiper Belt. He is entirely new to astrology, and entirely new to our spiritual awareness. He was the god of a little known people who have suffered a holocaust and great tragedy, but these people also had powerful spiritual beliefs that came closer to the `reality` of our existence than anything the western world was thinking at the time.

Knowing about the energy of Makemake brings a spiritual acceptance that embraces and opens our unconsciousness to living with him. He represents an important branch of existence that we need to understand so can we adjust, accept and harmonise with what the Divine wants from us. So despite Makemake's distance from us, both as a planet and as the spiritual deity of a very distant homeland, we need to pay him homage, reverence and thoughtfulness. To do this we need to learn about him, so here we go.....

How Makemake Was Given His Unusual Name

Makemake was discovered in on March 31st 2005 by a team of three astronomers, Mike Brown, Chad Trujillo and David Rabinowitz. Because it was Easter, they initially gave it the nickname of Easterbunny, and then called it that for the next 3 years because they couldn't think of any other name! The team were determined to choose names from religions and mythology outside of the usual ancient Greek and Roman choices, which broke with centuries of strict tradition and says a lot about the outspoken and maverick style of the guy in charge, Mike Brown. Mike says on his web site that he was careful and thoughtful in his choice of names, and we should be extremely grateful for that, because it has given us instant spiritual understanding. However, the inspiration to name this new planet was slow in coming. Because of the Easter connection, he had considered the pagan goddess Eostre, but then found out an asteroid already had that name. He considered rabbit gods (Easter bunny), including one called Manabozho, but said that none spoke to him and then left if for another year. Recognising that the project was soon to end and the public were loosing interest, the International Astronomical Union threatened to name the dwarf planet themselves, which finally made Mike Brown make a decision in 2008. He had a flash of inspiration and remembered the name of Easter Island in the South Pacific Ocean, which had been so-named because it was officially discovered on Easter Sunday in 1722. This gave the island and the planet the same birthday, 283 years apart. He searched mythology for the name of a god whilst remembering how masculine fertility and fecundity had overwhelmed him at the time of the discovery because he was going to become father to his first child.[1] Mike said that what he read about Makemake felt absolutely right to him at the time and I take that as confirmation that this deity and planet were really communicating with him, so I just know we have the right name.

The Story of Easter Island

There had to be some reason why the Divine chose, through astrology, to make this forgotten little island important, and I was curious as I ordered a mountain of science journals and books, initially thinking, "Nah….astrology's gone a bit weird here…can't be anything of interest on an volcano in the middle of the Pacific Ocean…" I opened the first one and slowly began to sit further and further upright. After about 3 chapters – the last one first because I am a Gemini and I always do that – I unplugged the phone and told my daughter to get take-outs for a month or two. (It actually took 3 months just to read the books!) This is a very sad and tragic story, which needs telling in full to honour the people. I can only hope the decision to name a planet after this poor little island's chief god will improve it's lot in life and perhaps Makemake hopes this too.

Easter Island has the most isolated position of any population in the world. It is 2,400 ish miles to the nearest significant land, Chile, and it takes 5 to 6 hours to get there by airplane. If you look at the little map, the dot in the middle of the circle is Easter Island, in the ocean in between Chile (South America) and Polynesia.

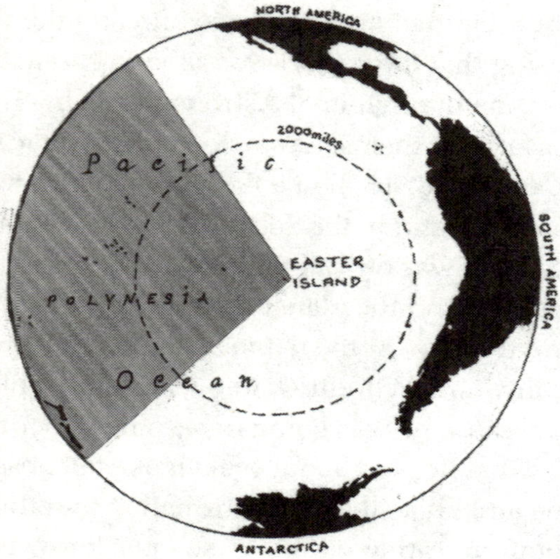

Illustration 9. *The dot in the middle of the circle is Easter Island. The dotted circle shows the emptiness of the 2,000miles around the Island. The shaded area to the left is the vicinity of Polynesia, which is a vast ocean and some small islands. (Adapted. See refs.)*

Polynesia is actually not a country, but a vast ocean, with a few tiny little islands in it. Two thousand years ago the people travelled vast distances across the sea as easily as we do now – but without modern navigational aids. How Easter Island got populated is a contentious issue and modern scientists get irate and scornful of each other's theories. There is evidence that explorers arrived on Easter Island from both Americas and Polynesia in the first millennium, which would make sense, since the island is in the middle of the two cultures. And although the Polynesians have certainly been the most obvious with the American influence being relatively weak, the collision and fusion of these two great peoples has made Easter Island a very special place with history, customs and beliefs that cannot be found anywhere else.

The Island itself is only 13miles by 11miles by 10 miles, in the shape of a triangle and it has a nice climate with an average temperature of around 20°C, albeit a tad windy. Each tip of the triangle is actually a volcano. First one popped up out of the ocean, then it's mate came along side and finally the last one was born. They huddle together in a group like a triple-peaked mountain, except that the peaks are volcanic craters filled with reeds and stagnant water. There is fertile grass growing on plains and slopes in between theses peaks. The volcanoes are 10,000 feet high from the seabed up, but only the top bits jut out of the sea and make up the island. Interestingly, (if you're into this sort of thing) the island sits on a fault line that goes all the way back to the Andes Mountains in South America (important because of the Nazca lines). This crack in the Earth's crust actually branches under Easter Island, which makes it a `hot spot`. There is so much molten lava coming to the surface of the Earth here, that basically the Island could either erupt or sink at any time and in fact there was a lava flow about 2,500 years ago.[2] Mysteriously, whole islands can suddenly appear or disappear under the sea in this area and myth has a god who levers them up and down.

Since 1888 the Island has been officially part of the country of Chile, with a population (c4,000 in 2004) that is heavily dependent on Chilean subsidies. However, the Island was colonised by a good percentage of Polynesians and confusingly it's people and language are called `Rapanui`, whilst the Island is officially called Rapa Nui locally.

In the late 19th century a holocaust brought about by Europeans and Peruvians nearly wiped out the **entire** population of 3,000+ in just a few years....... along with much of the indigenous spiritual knowledge, the structure and hierarchy of their culture and ancient artefacts. This is described fully later on.

These days, Easter Island is most known for what **couldn't** be destroyed and this has given us one of the biggest unsolved mysteries of our times. The Island is covered in hundreds of giant stone statues (called mo'ai) that were made to stand on equally giant stone built platforms around the coast. Some of these statues weigh many tons (20 to 270 tons!) and would have presented as great a challenge to the Islanders as the pyramids did to the Egyptians. Just as big a mystery is why they stopped producing them one day. Half of them were still being carved when one day the workers put down their tools and never went back! Another unsolved mystery is a strange hieroglyphic writing that has been found on this tiny island only and nowhere else in the world! The royalty and ancient priesthood who understood it were all killed, and missionaries destroyed most of it, although approx. 25 pieces of it remain to this day. The Polynesians never developed a writing system so where did it come from?

Other unusual features of the Island are ancient rock carvings and the caves the islanders used to live in at times. These were air bubbles and channels that formed in the cooling lava of the volcano, and the Island is riddled with them. So much so that Thor Heyerdahl commented "Easter Island is a world in two levels."[3] When he lived there in the 1950's there was a daylight world of reed huts and Christianity on the surface, with a Harry Potter world of skulls, ancient charms, superstitions, sorcery and mystery played out in secret caves in the dead of night. The Islanders knew two realities.

The Island's Different Names

It seems that one of the many injustices has been the name we call the Island. The earliest Islanders called it Te Pito te Henua which meant centre or navel of the world. The South American Inca capital also had a name that meant `navel of the Earth` so there is obviously some sort of connection between the two.[4] The Islanders liked the name because their volcano with a deep lagoon in it reminded them of a navel.

However, the French officials returning sick kidnapped Islanders in the middle 1860's made a confused and muddled association with another island, and finished up calling it Rapa Nui, the official Polynesian name it has today. However, the Spanish call it Isla de Pascua, and the English use the more affectionate name of Easter Island, which is the name I shall use because of the `Easter bunny` nickname which caused my astrological interest.

History of the Easter Islanders

The Outstanding Seamanship and Astronomy of the Ancient Polynesians

Our journey into an understanding of this deeply spiritual, brave and sensitive race begins with their seamanship and star reading skills. Advance scouts would leave Polynesian islands in ocean-going double-hulled canoes and travel thousands of miles to find new lands. Then they would go back and advise the others, who would then emigrate. Scientists have dismissed this simply on the grounds that these were savage primitives who couldn't have done this because they weren't sufficiently `evolved` and had no technological instruments. I'd just like to ponder on that point. Why do we insist that any humans that precede us could not have accomplished anything way beyond our abilities? I suppose it's because we expect that accomplishment is always built on and surpassed. But just as a man `peaks` and has his finest accomplishment, so do civilisations. Some humans write a book, or paint a picture, or climb a mountain or win a race, but can never go back and re-do it. Through an amazing burst of excellence they `push` something out, and then are content to recede and relinquish. So too with civilisations – no more pyramids for instance. The Polynesians had their finest hour of sea exploration, when for hundreds of years they honed skills that were later replaced by technology and western civilisation. Their scouts or navigators travelled across thousands of miles of ocean using a superior knowledge of the stars and ocean currents.[5] Their ocean going canoes were large, double-hulled and had out-riggers. They were big enough to house the emigrants, their animals and enough food and water for weeks at sea.

It seems that civilisations from the North and South American continent were also travelling the Pacific Ocean. Proof of this lies with crops such as the sweet potato, which came from South America, but was dispersed all over Polynesia. According to Clive Ruggles, the navigators were highly respected people who had high social status; maybe chiefs or priests. They used stars at night, and kept a mental image of the rising and setting positions of key stars and star groups from any position in the sea. They would also take into account the Sun, winds, currents, swells and clouds. Seabirds would tell them of nearby land or they would follow their migratory paths.[6] Captain Cook himself used the service of one of these navigators. The final evidence came when modern adventurers undertook these journeys and copied the conditions. In the 1950's a Swedish anthropologist called Thor Heyerdahl left the coast of South America in a copy of an ancient raft called the `Kon Tiki` and made it to a Polynesian island thousands of miles away, proving that early American civilisations could have had such a mastery of sailing. Then in 1975, a group called the Polynesian Voyaging Society also decided to prove what could be done and they launched a twin hulled canoe in which they have sailed hundreds of thousands of miles all over the Pacific Ocean using no modern technological methods – just sails and the stars. In 2007 this group was still going strong, and had made many voyages in many vessels, including a trip from Mangareva to Easter Island - a distance of 1,450 miles - in only 19 days! The captain on that voyage said:

> "We go to Rapa Nui in great humility and with respect for our ancestors, we go to rekindle the pride and dignity of our people and to reunite our ancient seafaring family."

After this historic journey one of the crew said:

> "Surrounded by an immense sea and forced to turn inward, we had discovered a harmony within ourselves and with the natural world. For all of us, this voyage had been a rare gift of mana."[7]

Present day recognition of Makemake symbolises the revival of this deeply spiritual people and hopefully their reconnection to the souls of their ancestors, the sea, the stars and the birds.

In fairness to the scientific argument though, I need to point out that respected ecologists and scientists have sold thousands of books on Easter Island to the public, declaring that:

> "it is extremely improbable that the island could have been reached more than once before the arrival of the Europeans."[8]

and

> "The chances of two such voyages managing to reach the same isolated speck just by heading west beggars belief."[9]

Phew! I will leave the scientist's comments to the opinion of the reader!

There is much heated debate and pontificating as to which races colonised the Island and when and I spent weeks reading all the different theories and getting very frustrated at how much they contradict each other. This type of disagreement and rivalry seems typical of the Polynesian race in general and there are claims that the islanders themselves became quarrelsome around the 17th or 18th century.[10] [11]

To give a short Island history, accurate enough for our needs, I'll use that given by Swedish anthropologist, Thor Heyerdahl, who lived on the island for several months with a team of archaeologists in the 1950's. It seems there were 3 epochs or periods. In the first, which lasted up to c.1200, explorers may have arrived from Chile or Peru bringing with them the skills to build massive platforms out of precisely cut huge stone blocks around the coast of the island. American Indians were also colonising islands in the Pacific Ocean and according to Thor Heyerdahl, could have reached Easter Island. There is actual evidence of Polynesian colonisation right at the beginning of the second period, circa 1200 to 1700.[12] One thing that is certain is that although the Island is small, the Island's population was made up of several different cultures and tribes which remained as separate as if they were in different countries; most particularly, it seems as if there was a big East – West divide. During this second period the different tribes started to carve the giant stone statues out of a single quarry and erect them on the large stone platforms.

The third period between the 18th and 19th century saw a *very* sudden end to the statue carving. During this period the Europeans arrived bringing diseases, slavery and murder. The priesthood and Island leaders were all killed or abducted along with most of the population. The social structure and sacred spiritual beliefs were consequentially destroyed.

The Island's Timeline:

I've put a timeline in here so you can keep referring to it; otherwise it gets a bit confusing. It is vague because there is much confusion, controversy and conflicting evidence surrounding it, but I have tried to stick to the main facts.

Between 400 – 1200AD First Epoch.
Early explorers arrive at different times from more than one place on the American continent. Perhaps early Peruvians, maybe a few American Indians plus some really early Polynesian settlers. Huge stone platforms were built. A wave of Polynesian colonisers arrived around 1200.

Between 1200 – 1700 Second Epoch.
Giant statues were carved. Makemake rock carvings. Possibly some European landings in the 1600's, but no written records.

1722 - 1800's - Third epoch.
Dutch Admiral Roggeveen officially `discovers` Easter Island and they murder 12 Islanders including leader. Upright stone giants are seen. Population reported to be 1,000's. From then on, Americans and Europeans are recorded visiting the island.

1570 – 1770 - At some point there may have been tribal feuding on the Island.

1774 - Capt. Cook lands and calls it Easter Island. Evidence that the some stone giants have fallen.

1840 -1864 – Last stone statue toppled?

1862 -1863 – A holocaust begins. Slave traders kidnap thousands.

1864 – The first Christian missionary arrives. What's left of the population dying from small pox, others were taken by missionaries to other islands.

1886 – Official population count 157. William Thompson arrives on the USS Mohican and stay for 12 days, writing the first reliable report.

1888 - Chilean ownership.

1915 – Official population count is 250.

Stories of the Islands First Polynesian Settlers

Island myths tell the story of how, in the first epoch, the first 300 or so Polynesian immigrants arrived on Easter Island. They were led over the sea by a king called Hotu Matu'a, who was escaping a bitter feud with a rival and had been advised by the great spirit Makemake that another Island could be found.

Centuries passed and we enter the 2nd epoch, at which point the Island was divided between Hotu Matua's clans on the west side and another tribe known as the `long ears` on the east side. (It was common for races all over that area of the Pacific Ocean to make big holes in their earlobes by inserting bigger and bigger things in them after piercing. Eventually their earlobes hung down to their shoulders. Strangely, teenagers in Birmingham were doing this in 2008)

Towards the end of this epoch, there was tribal fighting between the clans and between east and west in particular. It is told in tradition that skirmishes, raids and assaults did occur between the clans, mainly over women, honour and territory. The issues over fidelity must have been of great importance because there are many stories involving women going off with other men and tribal war breaking out as a result, but it seems the Polynesians males in general regularly took part in war games and one-upmanship.

William Thomson wrote of the Islanders in 1886 that:

> "Our guides were continually joking with each other, and we saw no quarreling or fighting. They are said to be brave and fearless of danger, but revengeful and savage when aroused."[13]

It is quite obvious that the earliest settlers were a resourceful, clever and courageous people, deeply respectful of Mother Earth, the spirits and their ancestral inheritance. Their clan or tribal way of life, competitive as it may have been, gave them something to be part of, they had a place, knew who they were and accepted both. Each clan had a class system of farmers, fishermen, priesthood, and royalty which supported their own statue carver's work. Some early contacts said the Island was flourishing and well farmed with Islanders who were robust, gregarious, good natured and in-offensive.

A Record of the First Contact, And the Terrible Outcome

The first recorded contact in 1722 describes how a single Islander in a canoe rowed out to Dutch ship at anchor 3 miles off shore. This would have been some kind of leader. He was described as fit, strong and completely naked with a goatee beard. During his time on board he spoke at length to the heavens, (I assume to the ancestors) and generally had a good time leaping and singing in gay merriment. When the Dutch landing party approached the shore they were given a rapturous welcome, and the Islanders had gifts of roasted chicken and bananas ready for them. It is then reported that whilst the natives were jumping for joy and exuding friendliness, (but also pilfering wood and cloth) trigger-happy sailors shot 12 of the Islanders…. including the previously mentioned leader! The islanders had carried no weapons – no spears, no knives….nothing. Hours after the shootings, a chief in white feather head dress, white cloth and white shell necklace quietly approached the Dutch offering homage and more bananas, sugar cane, young plants and chickens.[14] The Dutch left.

The Next 140 Years Were No Better

Can you imagine how the people on planet Earth would be affected if aliens dropped from outer space and behaved in the same way that the Dutch did? This episode must have had a shocking and devastating effect on the Islanders. Subsequent explorers also put on a big shows of firepower and gun salutes, which the Islanders were terrified of. Such was the impact that centuries later, with no written history to refer to, the Island's verbal legends still faithfully described all of these early encounters with outsiders. One contemporary author reports that

> "from 1722 to 1863 more than 1,000 islanders were gunned down or transported to their death by Europeans, North Americans and South Americans."[15]

It must have been at this point that the Islanders took to living in underground caves to hide from these raids. Thor Heyerdahl found evidence of this in the 1950's.

The Sexual Freedom of the Islanders

The women of Easter Island were famous for their beauty and grace. They wore no clothes and they enjoyed their seductive prowess and eroticism. Their attitude to sexuality was very different to ours. It was not taboo and they understood it to be a truly creative act that celebrated fecundity and the abundance of life. This went down well with the European and American sailors who worked in the Pacific at that time and the islanders mostly gave them a hearty welcome. From 1820 to 1860 hundreds of whaling ships called at Easter Island, mainly for the huge pleasure the women could give the men, and the crews reported that the Islanders were docile with the females sexually inviting. (According to Island practice, women could be leased out to other men and the Islanders had no problem with this. It had probably become necessary when there were few women compared to men in the early days. There would be trouble though, if the lady in question chose to look even further afield!)

The various ships would have left behind diseases, Christian doctrine, pregnancies and maybe even the odd sailor since the women were so keen to engage with these status-enhancing males. It is worth noting that throughout all the sailors' reports the worst atrocity any Islander committed against the explorers was to throw stones and steal. A report in NewScientist in 2006 said that artifacts previously identified as spearheads were actually agricultural implements and only a third of these had sharp edges.[16] This article also quotes an extract written in a

French journal in 1786 "a considerable population, with more beauty and grace than I afterwards met with on any other island;" So it was disturbing to read a report about an American whaling ship called the Pindos in 1822. After gathering up island girls for an all night orgy aboard their ship, the next morning they threw them all into the sea and then shot at the gathered crowd on the beach.

White skin was revered and apparently quite prevalent among the islanders – this was commented on often by the early explorers who were mystified by it. I have included a copy of an illustration drawn by one of the artists in Cook's party. He certainly looks more American or European than Polynesian.

Illustration 10. *This is a copy of a drawing done by a member of Captain Cook's party in 1774. Note the European type features and the elongated ear lobes.*

Polynesians had an exploring, fighting, macho image - very archetypally masculine. They both needed and respected strong leadership. If their leaders were perceived as weak next to the destructive might of the white aliens, then the leadership was challengeable and this might have brought about inter-island rivalry. When the Island women gave birth to white skinned males, courtesy of the European or American males, they were naturally challenging to the Island's royalty. Their shamans, chiefs and ancestral spirits had had undisputed authority, but that old system was crumbling, since the higher authority now was the white man with his guns, cloth and wood. Makemake was loosing his ground.

The power and authority of their own leaders would have been brought into question when compared to the brutal `magic` of these new white warriors and this would have caused a crisis of faith and leadership, so it is no surprise that some books suggest that tribal fighting broke out again around this time.

Another factor that may have changed the Islanders way of life after first contact was their mimicry. They saw the way the foreigners behaved and copied it. Commentators throughout the years have commented on the Islander's amenability and strong eagerness to please which meant they would morph to suit.

Thieving and pilfering was natural to the Islanders and they stole from each other all the time. It was a way of life, there was no shame in it and they even had a god to oversee it. They skillfully stole hats and handkerchiefs from sailors and these were important to the Islanders, since headdress denoted authority. (The chiefs and kings wore beautifully made and impressive head-dresses made from bird's feathers.) All the Islanders had secret family caves and here things could be kept in safety from the usual pilfering. The caves were protected by very elaborate ritual and taboo and signs of cannibalism were found in them in the 1955.

The Holocaust That Decimated and Killed The Population

The holocaust came in 1862 - 1886, when the Island's population was reduced from thousands to 155. In one recorded incident alone, Peruvians took up to 1,500 as labourers - one of them being the Island's king. Most of them died very quickly from diseases their immune system could not cope with and homesickness.[17] After international condemnation, it was decided to return the survivors to the Island. Only a handful survived the journey and made it back to their home. The smallpox they carried with them then started an epidemic that nearly wiped out the remaining Islanders. (If you're not crying yet, you must be a Scorpio!)

Two French Catholic missionaries were dispatched to the Island in 1866, one of whom frowned on Makemake and a yearly `birdman` competition in his honour, forbidding sexual practices, idols and ritual performances.[18] The word for penis was replaced by the word for wickedness and Island singing and dancing was stopped. They ordered the burning of all the carved wooden tablets with ancient island hieroglyphs on and the destruction of all pagan idols. This was an attempt to rid the Island of all it's spiritual heritage. European entrepreneurs then took over the stricken island, wrote themselves some contracts of ownership, fought bitterly with each other and finally made the whole island a sheep ranch. A different and popular missionary left for another island and took the many Easter Islanders who wanted to leave with him. To cut a long story short, a census in 1886 reported a list of 157 living on the Island, with the even lower figure of 111 survivors being reported in 1872.[19] I guess I don't need to say any more than that!

Easter Island is often held up as an example of ecological disaster by modern ecologists, who want to use the Island as a metaphor for potential world ecological disaster, righteously declaring that the Islanders had callously and mindlessly chopped down the last tree! Whilst I might be a bit of an eco-warrior myself, I have to say that I really think those authors may be missing the point!!

What was left of Old Easter Island and Makemake

The Islanders had suffered a savage destruction of their numbers through slave raids and imported diseases. Their king had been taken and the heart and soul had been taken out of their culture. Thomson wrote:

"Maurata, the last of a long line of kings, together with all of the principal chiefs of the islands was kidnapped by the Peruvians and died in slavery. Since that time there has been no recognized authority among the natives; every man is his own master, and looks out for his own interests."[20]

So the few remaining Islanders became directionless and vulnerable, as if the soul and the spirit of the people had died along with their leaders and belief system. The final `death` of Makemake came when the first missionaries announced sexuality and pagan gods to be evil.

William Thomson remarked "The amusements of the people were reduced to a minimum when the customs of their heathen forefathers were abandoned,"[21]

William Thomson's Report For the National Museum 1891

I've taken the time to write a few lines on this chap since his report struck me as being written by an observant, thorough and humorous person. In 1886 he was a paymaster of the U.S. Navy and spent 12 days on Easter Island (over Christmas) writing a long and detailed report for the United States National Museum, which is the earliest most reliable account we have. He got there about 20 years after the holocaust and spoke to important survivors of it. He therefore wrote the most uncontaminated report and for this reason I have used his account a lot. Other scholars arrived and wrote copious volumes another 20 years later, but by then all the survivors had died and there was no written record. Thomson has been accused of ransacking ancient archeologically interesting ruins, but he comes over as a precise and gentle man who at least wrote an insightful and painstaking document that gives us tremendous detail of the people, their culture and their history. He suffered considerable discomfort at times, but throughout this meticulous and studious report a wickedly dry sense of humour is occasionally evident. I found his description of the insects amusing, and thought it worth copying for you:

"From the earliest dawn of day to the close of the short twilight.......swarms of flies met us, prepared to dispute every foot of the ground. Whatever may have been the parent stock of the Polynesians, we came to the unanimous conclusion that we had discovered here the lineal descendants of the flies that composed the Egyptian plague, and can testify that they have not degenerated in the lapse of time. Fleas occasioned us more annoyance than the flies, because this industrious little insect was untiring in its attentions by day and night. They were found in numbers in all the camping places, and we seemed to get a fresh supply every time a halt was called."[22]

He was the only one who gave the Island it's real name and he says that no one else had thought to ask the natives what they called their home.

At the end of this chapter I have included a quote from William Thomson because I think it gives an insight into the soul of the man who wrote so carefully and thoughtfully of Easter Island.

Taboo and Mana

The spiritual system of Polynesia rests on these two principles or strengths, and most especially so on Easter Island. Mana is a supernatural power that can be wielded by special people, or can be won by those who go about things in the right way. These days we use the term `good karma` in England and it is not unlike a watered down mana. On Easter Island, the priesthood were the custodians and encouragers of mana, but it could be found wherever things were going really well; it meant they had been imbued with mana or good magic. Mana could also reside in a simple or sacred object.

Taboo refers to something that is not allowed. Taboo can be placed in objects that are left to warn people off, or it can be passed on by a verbal warning. The Islanders lived their lives wholly and completely according to taboo and mana and if the priesthood said something was taboo it was a no-go area. This would rule things like crop protection and bans on fishing to protect spawning fish.

The Islander's Spiritual Beliefs

The Islanders believed that a person's soul went to the place where the souls of the dead go – a spirit land that contained neither reward nor retribution; it just existed. Holes were built into burial places to let the soul out. Spirits also existed - greater spirits or lesser spirits, good spirits or bad spirits. They wandered the Earth and had influence over human lives, and could also communicate through dreams and visions. Some spirits became personal guardians to be called upon for guidance. Stone carvings in a variety of images represented a different genre of spirits - the household gods - and these could be consulted but they weren't worshiped. They were simply an access or communication portal to the other dimension of spirits. William Thomson found recesses for the statues of these household gods built into the construction of the earliest houses. He wrote down translations of Island hieroglyphs that give everything in existence an associated spirit or deity, from rocks to yams, grass, pain, bad smells, sea gulls, stars, luck and life! All things were imbued with a spiritual force, and a dialogue could go between humans and this energy.

The Islanders were controlled by superstitions and fear of the spirit world and it's supernatural power. To this end, they worked ceaselessly to appease the invisible forces, always trying to work in harmony with them. Fishhooks were made from the bones of dead fisherman in an effort to invoke his spiritual support and skill. Carved stones were buried under the threshold of dwellings to ward off evil spirits (an American Indian habit?) and the spirits were constantly consulted. Their priests, before the arrival of Christianity, would have been skilled in communicating with the spirit world, invoking magic, power and healing from it. The harmful spirits could invoke such paralysing fear that no one ever crossed them.

Makemake was in a class of his own - he was The Great Spirit, and when Islanders understood that early Europeans were praying, they joined in with cries to "Meke-meke".[23] Here in the western world, some of us are comforted by the belief that the spirit or soul of a dead relative lives on in the `other side` or `in spirit` and it comforts us to think we can still talk to them. The Easter Islanders whole-heartedly embraced this belief and took it to a much higher level. The ancestral spirits were protectors, guardians, masters, guides and constant companions to be consulted with in everything. We have translations of prayers that were offered to them to encourage abundance in health, food production and pregnancy, amongst other things.[24] The prayers mention the giant platforms, which were built before the statues and were positioned all around the coasts of the Island. They look like giant outdoor stages but were actually catacombs that held the bones of the ancestors. The statues were carved as a reminder and in honor of these ancestors; ornaments which perpetuated the memory and therefore kept their protection fresh and strong. The prayers said the spirits of the ancestors were "in the Sun", but they were also accessible to the living as protectors and benefactors. This reference to the sun does not have to mean sun worship. (Which is strongly denied by some) The element of Fire is a metaphor for the invisible realm of spirit – the life force of another dimension that underpins ours. In astrology the physical Sun is one of the things that represents spirit.

Ancient Spiritual Hieroglyphs called Rongorongo

In 1864 the first Christian missionary arrived and noted that surviving Islanders had stone or wooden tablets written in an ancient script called Rongorongo, which they kept in their houses and clearly treasured. The missionary obviously had a mission and set about ridding the small remaining population of it's heathen pagan religious beliefs. He encouraged the burning and destruction of all the Rongorongo texts, although approximately 20 pieces have survived.

The hieroglyphs of the script look like little figures, animals and objects, with a significant amount of fish and miniature `birdmen` figures, sometimes the same shape as the larger ones carved on the rocks, although each one can be altered slightly. The figures aren't the same as the Egyptian ones, but it is a similar concept and birds appear in both. Although having said, the birds are very stylized `birdmen` figures and don't look much like birds at all. If you compare with the later illustrations of the rock carvings of these `birdmen` then you'll see the similarity.

Illustration 11. *Copy of the Easter Island hieroglyphs called Rongorongo script.*

The Polynesians never developed a writing system, so unless we consider ancient myths of sunken islands and lost civilizations we are left with the mystery of where it came from. In 1939 a learned scholar claimed the hieroglyphs had similarities with some found in India, but this was scoffed at by others. Island myth states that tablets of the script were carried over the sea by the original pioneers. Thomson found a very old specimen of it in a really ancient tomb[25] so it's obviously not a recent thing. But if *where* this writing came from is a world-class mystery, then *what it means* is an even bigger one!

The script is carved in relief so it sticks out like Braille and when you reach the end of the line you have to turn the tablet as the next line is upside down to the first. This puzzles the experts greatly, but it seems to me that the similarity to Braille would make it easy to read in the dark. And if you are feeling it then you can't loose your place and skip a line if the lines either side are upside down. This would have come in handy for reading it in the caves at night or on a long sea voyage.

Information gleaned by Thomson suggests that bits of it contained origin myths and hymns that would be important to their rituals and spiritual well-being. There are lists of god/desses with their parentage and earthly associations, for instance. One or two recent scholars believe they have the key to reading this text, but since all such knowledge died along with the royal families and priesthood in the Island holocaust, no one will ever be able to confirm this. Fischer thinks that one of the pieces is solely about abundant prolific procreation - who copulated with who to produce what. There may be an emphasis on the male phallus and sex. According to Rjabchikov[26], another piece refers to water, darkness, burning, raining and different phases of the moon. There are references to Makemake as a Sun god, along with risings, settings and eclipses of the Sun. He believes there is information on Hailey's comet and a solar eclipse in 1531.

There is much discussion and evidence to do with this script on a Rongorongo website that any search engine will bring up, so those who want to read further can.

Longevity, Herbs And the Mysterious `Lomilomi` Healing Method

Apparantly one male Islander reached the age of 125, had milk white hair, could scarcely walk and had 23 children[27] – although not necessarily in that order! Thor Heyerdahl spoke of one who was 108 years old and William Thomson also comments on the longevity of the islanders; two of those known to him being upwards of ninety. When they weren't being murdered or kidnapped, the Islanders lived a long time!

Thomson observed that the 155 remaining Island survivors were in good and robust health. Apparently a cold virus would do the rounds every April, and walking on rocks would give them cracked feet, but apart from that the Islanders didn`t get ill. He suggested that physical regeneration came about through a healing therapy called Lomi-lomi. He wrote:

> "I may testify to the physical regeneration of this (pleasurable) manipulation. On more than one occasion I have thrown myself upon the ground, completely exhausted by over-exertion, and yielded to the dextrous kneadings and frictions and palmings and pinchings of those skilled in the treatment. The hard fisted native is by no means gentle in the operation, but with palms and knuckles vigorously tests every muscle and tendon, as well as every joint of the vertebrae until the exhausted patient sinks into oblivious somnolence."[28]

The practitioner claimed that this in itself wasn't enough, he was also applying "occult knowledge and supernatural power". This must be similar to Reiki, which originated in Polynesia (Hawaii). The Lomi-lomi by itself did not cause the longevity, but the free and copious use of it plus a healthy seafood diet obviously all contributed to a potential long life....however the big health news is this.....

Coinciding with Makemake's discovery, scientists also discovered a chemical called Rapamycin in the soil or rock of the Island which has incredible life enhancing properties, a real elixir of life. There is now a race to prepare it for human testing with the hope that it will cure most degenerative diseases.

There is an Island story that is a good example of how resilient and strong the men were. During the raiding and kidnapping missions in 1805, an American vessel kidnapped tens of Islanders after a ruthless and bloody encounter.[29] After 3 days sailing they allowed the victims on deck and immediately the men sprang overboard. It was assumed they all died when the ship could not find them and the incident was simply written into the ship's log. But Island legends gathered by missionary Sebastian Englert in the 20th century faithfully reported this story. How could the Islanders have heard of this? Certainly the ship did not return to report it. The legend came from one of the men who survived and swam back to the Island! He had survived the raid, 3 days in the hold of a ship and then a long swim back to his Island. Upon his return, his amazing story had become part of the Island's legends.

The "Festival of the Sea-Birds Eggs"

The early Europeans arrived to find a yearly competition that involved testing the strength, courage and stamina of the Island men. Thomson called it the "festival of the sea-birds eggs" whilst contemporary writers call it the `Birdman` competition. It centred on a knife-edge cliff between the sea and the crater of a volcano in a corner of the Island called Orongo. On one day of the year only, called the winter solstice (June 21st in the Southern hemisphere), the rising Sun just happens to line up exactly with Orongo and the volcano at the other end of the Island.[30] The winter solstice is a very important spiritual occasion for pagans the world over and throughout the centuries. Stonehenge in England focused on this special day. It marks the shortest day in the winter and therefore the beginning of the Sun's return to power and lighter nights. From this point on the Sun gains in strength and nature begins the march towards the Spring and Summer season; this symbolises re-birth and regeneration.[31]

On Easter Island the winter solstice also marked the beginning of the season in which the treasured Sooty Tern seabird returned. Islanders would go to Orongo and reside in special houses built for the festival, waiting for the arrival of the seabirds who came to lay their eggs on an off shore islet. As the race began, Island men would climb down a steep high cliff, swim the dangerous sea on a little raft made of reeds, climb up onto the rocky islet, collect an egg, and finally carry it back unbroken. Thomson wrote:

> "According to the ancient custom, the fortunate individual who obtained possession of the first egg and returned with it unbroken to the expectant crowd, became entitled to certain privileges and rights during the following year. No especial authority was vested in him, but it was supposed that he had won the approval of the Great Spirit Makemake and was entitled to receive contributions of food and other considerations from his fellows."

According to Thomson anyone could enter, most did, and factional fighting was common. (Many writers since Thomson have written different versions of this, but as I said before, he took his notes from the surviving 157 islanders and it is the most uncontaminated record. Subsequent writers may have been given embellishments since the Islanders so love giving the person in front of them a good story to please them.)

Associated with this competition is a symbol called a `birdman`, which has different forms and is carved all over the rocks at Orongo.

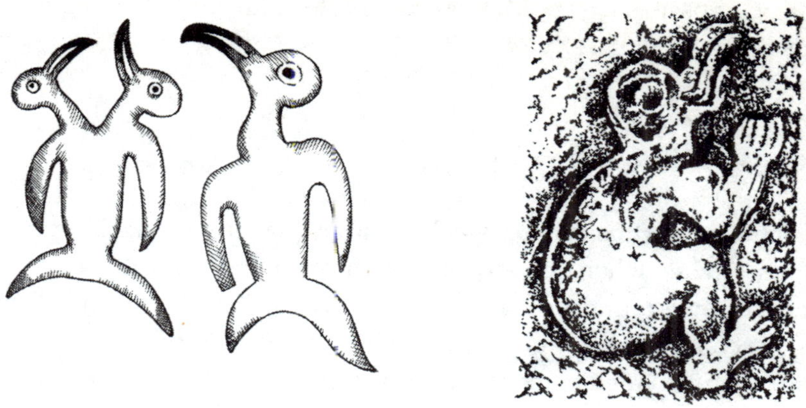

Illustrations 12 and 13. *Rock carvings and paintings of the birdman symbol. (If you see the beaks as ears, they look more like rabbits to me!)*

As you can see these have earlier and later forms and carvings are imposed over previous carvings by the dozen on the site. Along side the birdman images are those of a mask, which are meant to depict Makemake. (See later image) Thomson sees this Great Spirit as the patron saint of the competition.

Whilst the island's rock art is extremely prevalent around Orongo, it also exists elsewhere on the island - so much so that the whole island is considered to be a giant outdoor museum. Often the images carved are the same as those in the Rongorongo script – the island hieroglyphic writing - but which precedes which is not known.

The images sometimes bear resemblance to sea creatures and sometimes to constellations and stars, which would make sense, since without light pollution and high buildings the night sky would have been the most dominant feature of the Islander's lives. They may have been copying what they saw above them at night. The position of certain stars at different times of the year gave them information about weather and planting that was vital to food production.

A particular large boulder, found in a volcano crater, was carved with strange, spiritually imbued sea creatures, one of which had a human type head. Possibly one of Makemake's earliest images, showing his origins as the Great Sea Spirit.

Tricksters and Thieves

The Island rock art has an extremely strange quality – it can change into a different image when you look at it a different way. The mask of Makemake shown in the section entitled `Where Does Makemake Come From` is actually a man's genital region when looked at upside down. The birdman images can look like rabbits if you see the stylised beak as ears. The giant statues are just that until you notice how they copy the male phallus. This is more symbolism to add to the morphing nature of this culture. The Islander's obviously adored trickery and it must have been a good defence system for them. They had extremely impressionable natures, all commentators remarked as such, so their Polynesian competitive rivalry was played out in subtle ways. They were extremely adept at picking pockets and they *really* specialised in it.

But they weren't aggressive enough to steal guns, they stole hats and handkerchiefs. They would trick in other ways too, when they traded with the Europeans the sailors would find that a basket of sweet potatoes was actually a bag of stones with potatoes only on the top. They had a god to assist them in thieving whose name was Hiro and he was also the god of rain in Polynesia. Complex rules governed what was allowed and what wasn't, but suffice it to say that if someone transgressed then they had to submit to physical abuse from the victim without retaliating. Submission and acceptance were features of the Islanders mentality. Once this punishment was over, the matter was forgotten.

Interestingly the planet Makemake was going to be called Manabozho at one point, and he was a rabbit trickster god.

Illustration 14. *Mo'ai or stone statues of Easter Island. They were intended to stand on giant platforms as shown. They were on the coast but looked inward, towards the Islanders.*

Most people are aware of the giant stone statues of Easter Island. These are huge monoliths, carved out of one piece of volcanic rock and transported to the Island's 3 coasts to be placed on pre-existing large platforms, which were actually catacombs for the ancestor's bones. On average they are 13 feet high, weigh 14 tons (ish) and mostly faced inwards, with their backs to the sea. On the south coast alone there are 17 platforms in just 2 miles. A lot of the statues also had different-shaped hats carved out of red volcanic rock from a separate part of the Island. Although these also weigh tons, the Islanders placed them on top of the statues.

There are roughly 800 statues altogether with about half still in the production centre or quarry in one of the volcanoes. Some 300 had actually been transported to their coastal destinations, but about 50 were waiting to begin their journey and 50 were en route.[32]

In his book Aku-Aku, Thor Heyerdahl wrote of how he wandered about in the production centre in the side of the volcano, with 400 hundred unfinished giants gently watching him. He was moved by their ancient secrets and lofty silence. But most puzzling was the abandoned little stone picks that the workers had used to painstakingly chip away at the volcanic rock. They had thrown their tools down one day........... and never gone back. Why do that when they were only half way through the planned statues? Thomson said:

> "The images in all stages of incompletion in the workshops, and abandoned en route to the coast in various directions, indicate, that the work was suddenly arrested, and not gradually brought to an end."[33]

A theory could be that the carving stopped upon the arrival of the Europeans. Perhaps their murderous behavior implied that the protective power of the ancestors associated with the giants was not working, so producing more became futile? Or did the arrival of the Europeans spark off island feuding and tribal leadership issues, which took the work force away from the quarry? Was the statue factory production manager one of the islanders who was shot in the first contact? Or was it a combination of things?

One report states that each tribe had it's own road to it's own area of the island, and there were 7 different roads. In terms of the man power available, and the massive amount of construction that took place, the Islanders invested more time and energy per person than any other culture in the ancient world involved in the production of giant megalithic structures.[34] The report states that it must have taken about 500 years to do this amount of work and they could have been carving them up to the 1700's. However, another commentator, Fischer, guessed them to have been in production from 1250 to 1500. One thing is clear and that is they were getting bigger. The most recent was up to 28 feet tall, weighing perhaps 75 tons. The increase in size may have been one-upmanship; "My statue's bigger than your statue, nah!"

Although the Islanders had an intensely competitive instinct and strongly individual tribal identity, they must have co-operated in the carving of these awesome statues. Apparently a great deal of tribal pride and dignity was invested. The statues were obviously built to impress and protect.

Certainly the statues represented and honoured the spirits of the ancestors in a yang or masculine image, although there were a handful of female forms. Although they all looked roughly the same, there were some differences brought about by the carvers and clans involved. Thomson reported that surviving Islanders knew the names of each statue, and he tested them individually to be sure. He said they were "effigies of distinguished persons and intended as monuments to perpetuate memory."[35] He points out that they were not idols and they were not worshipped. The Islanders did not confuse them with actual gods. Importantly, although the Islanders carved lots of different wooden and stone images, there didn't seem to be any mini mo'ai statues and they never carved mo'ai faces on the rocks. A translator of Rongorongo said the text consisted of prayers to the good guardian spirits of the ancestors who were powerful protectors and represented by the "sacred stone pillars" or stone giants.[36]

When reading the Island mythology it is obvious that the similarity to the shape of the male phallus is every bit intentional. This people's love of the powerful male erection and the prowess and dominance associated with it was built into all their cultural expressions. Carved lines representing the hands and fingers of the statues emphasised and cradled it's male genitals.

Scholars like to guess at how these sacred stone pillars were moved miles from the quarry across the island and on this the Island myths were emphatic – they `walked`. The Islanders solemnly reported to Thomson that the statues walked about in the darkness, assisted their clans in competition and could prophesies.

It is ponderable why they were positioned on the coasts and faced inwards. They obviously weren't erected to frighten off those approaching the Island. They were enclosing the Island, forming a protective circle around it. They looked over the people and the people could look up a see the representatives of their ancestors looking back. The Islanders were at the centre and watched over. As suggested by the name of the Island, (`navel at the center of the world` or `navel of the deep`) the statues were contemplating the Island's own navel.

Why then, did they get knocked down in later years? The main theory is that the Islanders pushed each other's statues over to nullify the ancestral power or really peeve their neighbours during tribal skirmishes. Theory number two involves a legend called `The Fall of The Stone Statues`. In it, we are told, "The statues fell to the ground. The wind blew, there was lightening, thunder rumbled in the night. The next day the statues had fallen."[37] Interesting that there should be a story about them being brought down by a storm, when surely the more exciting story would have been about warrior wars and heroes. It just so happens that in 1746 the most deadly earthquake and tsunami for 200 years destroyed the entire port of Callao and city of Lima on the coast of Peru, which after all is the closest land to Easter Island.[38] Whilst looking at one particular platform, William Thomson noted that:

> "The ruined condition of these solid specimens of architecture, with the overthrown images and immense deposit of loose boulders on the surface of the ground, are strongly suggestive of earthquakes and volcanic eruption."[39]

Such an earthquake happened again in 1960, and the resulting 26 feet high tsunami carried 15 statues weighing approx. 30 tons each 500 feet inland,[40] so it obviously happens. (There is a question mark over the deity responsible for the tsunami of 2004 and at this point the jury is still out as to whether Makemake or Sedna have patronage.)

Perhaps the two theories can be combined and tribal leadership upheavals happened as an earthquake knocked over some of the statues and this kicked off a spate of retaliatory statue felling. We are never going to find this out for sure. The strong, superior, silent statues will keep their secrets into eternity.

Where Does the God Makemake Come From And What Does He Represent?

The word Makemake (written Meke-meke by Thomson) obviously contains a duplication of one word and this is apparently an emphasis, a superlative implying a higher degree of quality. Thomson was told

Meke-meke was `the Great Spirit of the Sea` and certainly the earliest images of him implied he swam in the sea or moved in the Ether.

Makemake's prominence as creator god of fertility belongs to Easter Island only. Just 64 square miles of planet Earth. The usual chief Polynesian gods weren't especially acknowledged. According to legend, one of them called Hiro, god of rain and thieves was accepted. Another of them, Tangara, arrived but was murdered on the beach. The odd commentator thinks that two others may have been merged into Makemake. But in truth, it is a mystery! How and why did the Islander's have a god that didn't appear anywhere else?

Sometimes the need for a certain god/dess is driven by a surplus or lack of something in that culture. The sensitivity of a population anywhere to the lack of water for instance, or the abundance of seafood, will guide them to identify god/desses that can represent these matters. Another thing that influences the relevance of local god/desses is the local sky. All ancient civilisations the world over used the moving canopy of the night sky and planets as their television set, newspaper and internet connection. And just as these media things influence our lives now, so the busy and vibrant stars influenced the ancients. The god/desses were and are represented by stars and planets which look as if they are moving around and stories were concocted to explain the effect this would have on people's lives. Now take a look again at the map of Polynesia at the front of this chapter. The distance from Hawaii to Easter Island is 4,600 miles, which is more than the distance from England to Alaska, but more importantly the sky that can be seen on a regular yearly basis in the Northern hemisphere (Hawaii) is **different** to the view from the Southern Hemisphere (Easter Island). Different stars were rising and falling just before the all-important Sunrise. Stars that rose ahead of the Sun were **most** important to **all** the ancient civilisations. Now put all that together and it is easy to see why different Polynesian islands (Hawaii and Easter Island) had some differing god/esses. The needs, outlook and culture of the people were different.

Because Easter Island sits in the middle of Tahiti (Polynesia) and Chile (South America), it was and is a fusion of East meeting West. Largely because of the sea travel undertaken by the early Americans and

Polynesians in the first millennium, some things such as the habit of lengthening earlobes, the sweet potato (called kumara in Peru and Easter Island), a plant called the bottle gourd and megalithic stone work just swirled around that whole quadrant of the planet. An important early city in South America and Easter Island both had a name that roughly meant the "Navel of the Earth". DNA from chicken bones found in Chile and dated to 1400 was the same as the DNA from chicken bones found on 2 South Pacifican islands even further away than Easter Island.[41]

Easter Island was where Polynesian and the Americas influence fused. The Polynesian influence was the clear winner, but the South American influence was just enough to make some things unique to Easter Island only. So enter Makemake. Unheard of in South America or Polynesia. An ingenious and mysterious Easter Island solution to the presence of two great spiritual dynasties and local needs. There were some similarities between the spiritual beliefs of the Peruvians (South America) and the Polynesians. The ancient Peruvians also deeply revered their ancestors and as the number of ancestors increased, so did the ritual demands. Both races recognised the importance of a cluster of stars called the Pleiades, which used to rise before the Sun in the morning.[42]

To understand this, you have to imagine what it was like to be entirely dependent on the success of your own crops. No shooting off to the local supermarket if your potatoes failed to grow. You lived or died according to the success of the seed potatoes you were planting – it had to be right, and because the ancients had no weather forecasts they used a more reliable method – they watched the stars! The Island's priesthood knew that if the Pleiades looked dim around the winter solstice they needed to plant at a different time from the usual to adjust for the coming season of reduced rainfall. Scientific research carried out in 1999 proved this to be true. The poor visibility is caused by a different pattern in very high clouds, which changes the weather pattern for the growing season 7 months hence.[43]

Easter Island didn't have any streams or sources of fresh water, and rain drained away quickly, falling through the volcanic rock and myriad caves. So their all-important potato crops depended on a planting strategy that made best use of coming rainfall. Their neighbours in South America had this forecasting system and it would have been passed on to the Island's priesthood and elders by the explorers going back and forth. The brightness of the Pleiades on the all-important winter solstice would have told them when to plant to take best advantage of next season's rainfall. But although the Pleiades and the winter solstice were of crucial importance for timing purposes, the real spiritual support and power for growth and re-generation came from Makemake.

A clue to Makemake's origins comes from Polynesian mythology containing a lesser-known deity called Makalii or Makarika. The Pleiades (along with another group of stars called Hyades) were known as Makalii or Makalii's nets. (There is a myth that the Polynesian rat gnawed through these nets, but she wasn't in trouble because she was Makalii's sister.)[44]

It is easy to see how Makarika became Makemake and usurped the usual Polynesian creator god who may not have been practical enough for Easter Island needs. They needed a creator god of abundance and fertility to join Hiro, god of rainfall, who was also connected with the star cluster of Pleiades. It is also easy to see how this happened when we understand that this all-important information about the weather could ensure a bumper crop or a failed one. It would mean life and death on an island with no fresh water and a sexually indulgent population who enjoyed procreating.

Amazingly, Easter Island has a natural cliff top feature which the Islanders exploited to be able to tell when the exact day of the winter solstice was, and the priesthood couldn't have failed to notice that the season of the return of the seabirds to nest and lay delicious eggs was also heralded by this day. Makemake's image was carved all over this feature, and the `Festival of the Sea-Birds Eggs` was arranged around it. I guess this date must have also influenced the seasonal ban on fishing imposed by the priesthood to allow stocks to breed. Turtles were regarded as sacred, as many rock carvings testify, and they also have ancient symbolism with the Pleiades. They, like seabirds, crossed thousands of miles to lay eggs on Easter Island and they were protected by the taboo of the priesthood, which meant the number killed was strictly controlled. Turtles bridged the two worlds of deep sea and land and as such could be messengers of the Great Sea Spirit, one of Makemake's titles. They could also assist souls to the next dimension. Their egg laying cycle depended on new and full moons, which the priesthood could predict.[45]

What did Makemake Look like?

William Thomson gave us the most important Makemake image, but surprisingly I seem to be the only one who thinks so! This may be because his report did not become a book and was not readily available to the public. Since then, scholars have concerned themselves with other knotty little issues such as statue erection and ecology, and knowledge of Makemake has been consigned to one or two brief mentions in Easter Island books in which they use one of the many bird man carvings to represent him.

However, William Thomson says "According to the natives, this symbol was intended to represent the god `Meke Meke,` the great spirit of the sea." He then refers to the following illustration that he drew himself:

Illustration 15. *A copy of an illustration drawn by William Thomson in 1886. This image was carved on a rock.*

He goes on:

> "The general outline of this figure rudely carved upon the rocks, bore a striking resemblance to the decoration on a piece of pottery which I once dug up in Peru, whilst making excavations among the graves of the Incas. The form is nearly identical, but except for this instance, no similarity was discovered between the relics of Easter Island and the coast of South America."

(I then spent a very boring night trying to find similar images on Google. 3 glasses of wine and the hiccups later, I'd found 2, but that hardly constitutes prevalence. I decided that I'm going to go to the South Pacific to carve something silly on a rock and leave it for someone to find in 2,000 years…It'll drive them mad!)

The Islanders didn't make pottery, so none could have been taken to Peru. The explanation has to be that 1 or 2 items with this image on made their way *from* Peru. William Thomson sketched his old Makemake image over 120 years ago, and it may have eroded since then, because it is not used in the recent Easter Island books. However this face is very similar to that of an early epoch statue unearthed by Thor Heyerdahl in the 50's. Thomson's ghostly image is so ethereal and ambiguous, it suggests many different possibilities and perhaps that is the point…….it is all things; neither a land animal, nor a sea animal nor a spirit from another realm – Makemake is everything. At some point the face of this image got reduced to a mask, and masks of one form or another are common in Polynesia.

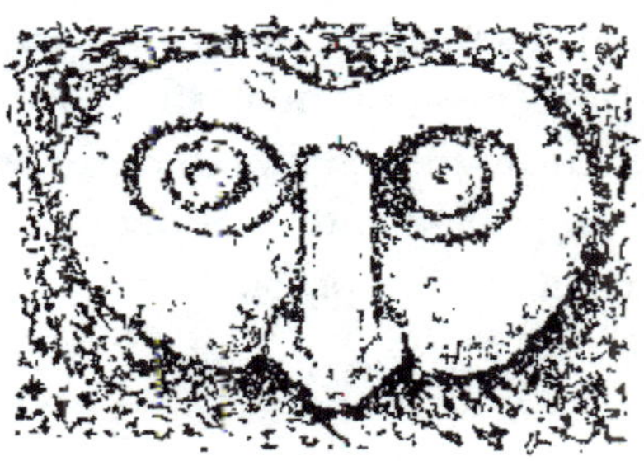

Illustration 16 *This `mask` rock carving of Makemake is the more recent and most prevalent image of him.*

However, most commentators now associate Makemake with the more modern of the birdman images (see the illustrations in the previous `Festival of the Seabirds` section) which are superimposed over the earlier, more spirit-like and ethereal images. The side-on shape of the birdman image has similarities with those on other Polynesian islands.

So there we have it, the very earliest image of Makemake, with the evidence seeming to point to a little bit of Peruvian connection as well as a Polynesian pedigree.

The Meaning of Makemake to the Islanders

Makemake the Great Sea Spirit

These days, it is said that Makemake was the creator of humanity, the god of fertility and the chief god of the birdman ritual. Thomson said the survivors called him the Great Sea Spirit, and implied he had a big connection with the ocean. This is only natural since the tiny island was surrounded by ocean. It seems that this ocean was more abundant than we previously realized and the Islander's had a lot to thank Makemake for. In 2008 it was reported in NewScientist that the area north of Easter Island had been found to be one of the richest and best places on the Earth for large ocean predatory fish such as marlin, tuna and shark.[46] This has surprised the scientists who put it down to a perfect sea temperature.

Another amazing report came out in 2009, when scientists found that storms or changes to the usual annual weather events of the eastern Pacific had a dramatic impact on the quantity of important fish YEARS after the event. This is due to the amount of nutrients that swirl up from deep water, boosting stocks and breeding potential. It says "The effect of El Nino events on fish has probably been observed for millennia….." and

> "After discovering these relationships between decades long fluctuations in fish and climate all over the world, scientists are now probing back in time to see if similar relationships exist on the order of centuries and millennia."[47]

So storms and tsunami`s could be trusted to improve the amount of available seafood over the following years. It is likely that the Islanders attributed these extreme weather events to Makemake, since he was the Great Sea Spirit and capable of creating them.

Another of his great gifts to the Islander's was `The Festival Of The Sea Birds` which revolved around the winter solstice and was used to judge the brightness of the star cluster called the Pleiades. As I said earlier, this would describe the strength and timing of the El Nino rainfall and winds the following year, and tell them the best time to plant. Guided by the priesthood, who understood nature's way and how to work with sea conditions and projected breeding patterns and then used taboo to control when to plant or fish, the Islander's were able to enjoy Makemake's abundance whilst living with nature. If they observed the festivals, traditions and social restrictions; the Islanders must have had good crops, bird eggs and prolific seafood. Perhaps the recently discovered Rapamycin chemical elixir also boosted the virility, stamina and profusion of everything on the Island. The problems came with the breakdown of the social order and loss of spiritual connection that taboo, mana and the priesthood had kept in good working order. The murder, slavery and Island holocaust replaced the priesthood that could `read` the brightness of Pleiades and enforce the ritual taboo that protected the people. Makemake's importance was *really* lost when the Island population was reduced to 111 survivors, none of whom were the priesthood or elders who knew what that importance was.

Makemake as a Sexually Bawdy Deity

Father Sebastian (a later Island missionary and a deeply spiritual man) explained how Makemake began as one thing and morphed into another and I think there is no doubt that whatever Makemake was in the first millennium, in the 19th century he was a sexually bawdy and competitive deity. This was obviously supported by the Rapamycin chemical that has been tested to increase virility and libido, although it was also completely in keeping with the strongly competitive macho image so prevalent in this quadrant of the planet.

World myths often tell us of how new ways open up when things are looking bad. The population, race, or hero/ine recovers the heart and mind to go on because of the arrival of a bawdy joker who brings humour, mirth or at the very least distraction, just when the lowest ebb is reached.[48] Sexual innuendo or lascivious comments are common and Makemake fits right into this role. Such a story can be found on the Marquesas Islands, which are Polynesian islands within striking distance of Easter Island. This story can also be found in the mythology of Greece, Japan and Egypt, which is an example of how myths seem to be hard wired into our DNA and emerge when triggered by a certain event.[49] When the Islanders had all but been wiped out of existence, Makemake became a smutty comic of bawdy sexual innuendo, which was useful both as a reminder to procreate and replace the lost population, but also to provide something to snigger about. Makemake was naturally equipped to provide the sexually suggestive innuendo because he had serious connections to sex in the first place. Maybe his energy *is* the Rapamycin. William Thomson points out that the Rongorongo script contains much reference to Makemake and the female vulva, which represents the birth of a person.

The hieroglyph Rongorongo script seemingly contains lots of reference to deity and the creation, and since the little figures are often like the rock art that islanders identify as Makemake, some assume the god of the hieroglyphs is Makemake. The following was written by a scholar in an article printed in the Journal of the Polynesian Society in 1939. He says

> "It was perhaps the emphasis on sexuality in these tablets that made the basis of the Easter Island belief in their virtue as aids to conception. There are other religious cues of the characters; the great god Makemake is very often repeated; it is made of bird, mammal, sometime human and fish; it takes varieties of forms. He is the representative of power; he is seated on his throne, with symbols of royal authority in his hands; his head touches the heavens and he wields the lightning and thunder"[50]

> "Makemake's energy supported numerous different forms of emotions connected with procreation and fecundity. He was a stimulation to fertility, impregnated with the passion of procreation and the idea of reproduction which was never out of the minds of the people."[51]

A more recent theory suggests that in old Rapanui language Makemake means "tumescent (of the phallus)".[52] I looked up tumescent, and it means swollen or becoming swollen.

To get a better impression of the prowess and abundance that Makemake can endow we need to take into account the easily expressed feelings of Mike Brown, the planet's discoverer. His wife was pregnant at the time and his male pride in his fertility was apparent for all to see - he talked of his wife's pregnancy and the birth of his daughter frequently.

Physical Prowess and Competition

According to Thomson, Makemake was always celebrated at the important island festivals through sporting competition. Events such as stone, javelin and net throwing or the yearly race and swim to collect the bird's eggs were common and the Islander's loved them. The celebrations would revolve around such events changes in seasons or the anniversary of the arrival of the mythical first king. Losers were agreeable, easily resigning themselves to their fate and whatever loss they had to bear. It is a remarkable feature of the Islander's natures, that their spiritual beliefs meant that they happily surrended to that which prevailed.

Birds As Sacred Beings and Messengers of the Divine

Feather headdress donated rank or statesmanship as it did in many cultures around that quadrant of the planet. Birds had supreme importance in all the major spiritual dynasties. A glance through Egyptian, North American Indian and Eskimo mythology will testify to this, to mention just a few. Birds held a special place because they could communicate with the sky god/desses and the people on Earth. Birds could carry the soul into the other realms. They would disappear for months and then reappear to nest and lay eggs, so it was no wonder that the Islanders associated them with travel to other realms and the return to Earth to begin a new cycle. Birds in England announce seasonal cycles with the dawn chorus, which fades in late summer and autumn but gears up again around the winter solstice and builds to a deafening crescendo in spring. Try waking up early enough to go outside and listen to it as often as you can - their song will talk to your soul. The Easter Islanders were reported to have seabirds landing on their shoulders; their biggest yearly ritual venerated them and they used them to navigate thousands of miles across the ocean. Birds were very special.

The Magic of Shells and Feathers

Shells and feathers were given the highest reverence as ornamentation, with only island kings and priests wearing particular ones, and others being reserved for special events. The spirit of the sea creature or bird remained in it's bones or shell or feathers, so they gave the ability to be closely identified with these sacred and spiritual representatives. As feathers and shells protect their occupants, so they might confer the power of protection to their new wearer. Such was their belief that the power of the spirit remained in the bone, they would make fish hooks out of the bones of dead fishermen or birds. Turtles were especially highly prized and protected, and they feature often in the rock art. Turtles are associated with the Pleiades as are the nets that catch fish. White items were the most revered, but red was also an important colour for them, and this might have been because the Sun glows red before it appears or disappears over the horizon. Since the Sun's light is actually white during the day, the Sun is always one of these two colours. The god of feathers was called Era Nuku and wherever feathers are placed he keeps away challenging spirits and brings good luck.

How Will Makemake Help Us in the 21st Century?

Eastern Spiritual Beliefs

When Mike Brown made the courageous decision to break away from the century old tradition of naming newly discovered planets after Greek and Roman gods he did something very special for the human race. He made the West turn to look at something else. He made us look to the East.

In Eastern shamanic beliefs all things on Earth - rocks, plants, water and animals are imbued with magical power, force and energy. This concept has been alien to the West during the reign of Christianity, which worships a single god and not nature. In Christianity we lost our relationship with the environment. Christian missionaries spent years trying to stamp out ancient sacred feminine traditions, which all had deep connections with the environment and natural rhythms. But now quantum science is telling us that the sub atomic particles that make up the molecules in rocks, plants, water and animals are indeed made of a magical force or energy. They are not just inert, lifeless, solid bits. The Easter Islanders knew this from the inside of their souls. They fully and totally lived this spiritual understanding.

The unique and special skills required to blend with the celestial stars and paddle according to their movement, or blend with the ocean's currents and understand instinctively what they mean, forges and hones an attunement with nature which we will probably never be privileged enough to know.

The people in this quadrant also understood the presence of the other dimensions, which science now finally accepts exists. They understood different planes or dimensions, where souls and spirit exist as pure energy. Spirit could be communicated with through ancestors who were nearer to the god/desses or deity because they had passed over. To the Islanders, the other realm was an ever present, strong reality and they were always in dialogue with it. When the first contact was made, the Island Chief was noted to be constantly talking to either his guardian spirit or Makemake. In 1955, Thor Heyerdahl wrote that the

Island Mayor was always consulting with his spiritual guides and he would talk to them and then pause and listen. When the Mayor's granddaughter died in an accident he was comforted by the knowledge that she could now help the family from the `other side`.

The fundamentals of all these Eastern spiritual beliefs will become known and important to us in the future. There is a huge shift in our spiritual consciousness taking place, and it is a move towards Eastern or Polynesian spirituality.

Our Exploration of the Cosmos and a Gung-ho, Seafaring Spirit

Whilst Makemake has a gentler, submissive, watery side; he also represents the spiritual element of Fire and supported a race with competitive, fearless confidence and strong connections to the realm of spiritual support and gnosis. They had a curious, adventurous, gung-ho energy. It is this pioneering spirit that first put mankind in an aircraft and then a space rocket, or in this case an ocean going canoe to sail or paddle thousands and thousands of miles.

That journey exists for us again now. As a human race we are reaching out with all the curiosity of those early Polynesian explorers, expanding and crossing new horizons at a rapid rate. So we will need the same gut instinct and trust that the Cosmos, the God-ness, the ancestors and Mother Nature gave to the Polynesian scouts and pioneers. Early astrological indications seem to suggest that Makemake represents kidnapping and piracy, surely an audacious practice requiring skillful seamanship. The Islanders were kidnapped by the thousand, so this does make sense.

The Theme of Duality Occurs Throughout All Kuiper Belt Planets

It is interesting to see this concept reinforced again by the appearance of a dwarf planet in our solar system whose meaning resonates with it. The story of Makemake's home, Easter Island, includes many dual realities. This contrast was echoed in the population, who occupied 2 distinct halves of the island. The island straddles the edge or end of the

Polynesian empire, and edge or end of the New World Empire. The islanders lived at the centre of two worlds. The Spanish and New World civilisation was stretching west and the spread of civilisation from China and the Far East was spreading east. Easter Island was therefore, true to it's ancient name as the navel or centre of the World.

In the 20th century, when the Islanders took on Christianity and their dearly beloved minister Sebastian Englert, they led two spiritual existences with two religions. By day they prayed and sang in the island church and by night a Harry Potter world of spirits, demons, ancient taboos, human skeletons and secret caves sprang into life - all very dark and very secret. They took ancient charms, superstitions and sorcery in their stride; it was part of life and living. Christianity was another thing apart and they easily handled both. There is a surface grass level to life......... and an underground cave level to life.........one underlies the other. The islanders easily absorbed and exaggerated the dual nature of their lives. Their other dimension was the realm of ancestral spirits who communicated with them and could help or hinder.

All this can be seen as a metaphor for the dimension that we live in and the unseen `dark` or invisible dimension that science has now proven intertwines with ours. Makemake is the spirit that abides in this other realm, but can be called upon to assist in this one. The Islander's acceptance of both world's fitted well with general Polynesian beliefs, where the other dimension exists in all things in our realm.

The clear concept of duality or twosome could be found in the issues that the ancient Peruvians had about twin births. One was seen as ok but the second was regarded as trouble. One was dark and one was light. It could represent an un-conscious part of us that seems to work against us at times because it has a different agenda and therefore might be termed as `trouble`.

Rabbits and More Rabbits!

The island rock carvings of birds and `birdmen` look uncannily like rabbits if one sees the beak as ears. And that makes sense of the body shape – a dead rabbit, put on it's side, is much more that shape than a bird! Go back and have a look at the illustrations again, can you see a rabbit? Records say that rabbits had to be introduced to Easter Island; they are not indigenous to the Island, so a rabbit symbol makes no sense at all. The only connection with rabbits is the nickname that the astronomer initially gave the planet – Easter Bunny and the fact that it was nearly called Manabozho after the indigenous North American rabbit trickster god. Yet an astrologer's instinct still says rabbits! Whilst I was writing this chapter I noticed and bought rabbit meat to eat which is something I would never normally do, and the description of the island caves and tunnels given by Thor Heyerdahl kept reminding me of rabbits and burrows. The Islander's had at some stage built houses that were deeply embedded in the earth like burrows and only had tiny entrances.

The Islanders did have plentiful edible rodents however and these were very much part of their lives and stories, so maybe this explains it. Or maybe the rabbit feeling has something to do with the legendary sexual activity and fertility of rabbits or the mythical transformative and magical powers. Legend and folklore always connect rabbits and hares with renewal, fertility and rebirth and this is completely in accord with the lusty sexual proclivity of the ancient Islanders and their beloved Makemake.

Makemake Brings Abundance. Illusion or Not?

When Admiral Roggeveen landed for the first time in 1722 he wrote in his official log at the time "The island was found to be destitute of trees, but with a fertile soil producing bananas, potatoes, and sugar-cane of extraordinary thickness." Then somebody else reports him as saying "singular poverty and barrenness". Who is right? There are many other such references to the abundance on the Island, for instance: "and a soil which with very little labour furnished excellent provisions"[53] It's possible that the Islanders habit of saying what the person in front of them wanted to hear, also stretched to the Island itself. The visitors saw what they expected to see. If they had an expectation of barrenness, that's what they got. There is something of an illusional quality about the energy. Things looked plain on the outside, but underneath there is mystery. Was there abundance or not? This energy may represent `The Secret`. The esoteric spiritual knowledge that if you want something you have to truly believe and expect it and then it will become. You can constellate or magnetise it into your life.

Another explanation for the Islander's ability to feed so many on relatively little land may have been their expert management of the land in full harmony with nature and natural law, or, once again, back to Rapamycin which may have worked on the land too. Whatever, they produced far more per acre than we do now with all our chemicals.

Comparison of the Microcosm of Easter Island to the Macrocosm of Planet Earth. Over Population and De-population.

William Thomson wrote in his report:

> "The traditions assert that the island was in former ages densely populated, and the legends are supported by the gigantic works of the image and platform builders......there is every reason to believe that the people were numerous enough to severely tax for their support the limited area of ground available for cultivation."[54]

The Islanders lived in harmony and accord with nature, in mysterious dialogue with earth, animals and sea creatures and perhaps we would regard how they grew crops and fed themselves as miraculous.

However, present day ecology alarm bell ringers have used the Easter Island story as a warning of what could happen to our planet and it is hard not to think along those lines when one reads all the `expert` books on the subject. Some that I read really over-stretched and speculated about what may have happened to the island's ecology before the arrival of European contact – something that science shouldn't really do! Some of it may be valid, but there were reports that were not really fair. For instance, in 1886, after the Islanders had been reduced to a population of 111, the Europeans landed horses, 100 cattle and 18,000 sheep on the Island that roamed freely and ate the whole Island. By the time Thor Heyerdahl got there in 1955 the sheep had eaten through so much of the flora, there were only 47 varieties of plant life left! A later scientist then leaped on this fact and used it to claim that the early Islanders had decimated their island.

However, since 2004 scientists have slowly been changing their previous doomsday ecocide allegations and this is cause for celebration. Perhaps Makemake has returned to help tell the *real* story of the Islanders before the holocaust.

In the meantime, there are still un-answered and lingering questions about over-population and de-population. Thomson found thousands and thousands of skeletons on the Island, and a great deal of housing. He commented on the mystery of how on earth that many people lived on the island with no obvious fresh water. The Islanders had found or knew a way.

In 2009 Makemake's energy was really heightened astrologically for a while and this allowed a glimpse of what the represents. One of the things that came up was Sir Richard Attenborough's new position as patron of the Optimum Population Trust. An organization that recognizes that planet Earth cannot support un-fettered population growth. It seeks to support voluntary population controls before the population is brought under manageable numbers by plague or starvation and lack of resources.

Some scientists speculate that there is a Mother Nature has a natural `feed-back` loop that will kick in and automatically reduce the population of the planet one way or another. They point to the rise and fall of great civilizations and ask if they succumbed to this natural mechanism. If you have ever kept fish in a pond you will know that they regulate themselves in some way. When the optimum population is reached, one or two obligingly die so that the staus quo is maintained.

Since Makemake presided over a massive de-population of Easter Island, it is likely that he represents these things in the collective and these issues will become a focus of world attention

Makemake and Pandemics.

Linked closely to the de-population of Easter Island is the wildfire spread of infectious disease, which were brought to the early Islanders by the Europeans. Even in Thor Heyerdahl's visit in the 1950's, the arrival of the yearly navy ship from Chile would initiate a round of influenza, normally resulting in some fatalities. It was apparent in 2009 that Makemake's energy still resonates with the issue of pandemics. Ironically though, on this occasion, the infectious influenza began in the Americas, (Mexico) and spread to Europe. In the 1800's it was the other way round.

Planetary energies, or god/desses, can symbolise a surplus or proliferation of whatever it is they represent, or they can symbolise a lack or loss of it. So therefore Makemake can represent an actual pandemic, the threat of one, of the recovery from one. Now you know who to talk to about any of the above!

Has The Great Sea Spirit Returned to Guide Us Into Proper Use of the Seas Again?

Religious dynasties of the last two thousand years have taken us away from nature and the belief of a sacred, divine force in all things. We stopped believing that the Universe was a web with all things dependent on it and each other, and all as important. We believed that as humans we were somehow above and separate to the animals, the wind, the sea and the earth. That we did not need to observe and honor the ways of the ancients and their affinity with Nature. Makemake's return symbolizes a return to his ways.

It was reported that the Islanders imposed their own fishing restrictions, and did not fish for tuna between the months of May and September[55] and I have already mentioned their harmonious relationship with the seabirds. These are just two examples of how they understood their environment.

It is hardly necessary to remind the reader that we have not been so successful in properly harvesting the fish stocks of our oceans and the situation has been absolutely dire in recent years. However, marine conservationists are at least now aware that there is a problem and how it can be fixed. We will need to work with nature and the seas, treasuring and honoring their fragile, sacred power. However, the whole issue is subject to politics, international co-operation and human greed without reverence. Although we can no longer stand in front of the rising Sun on the winter solstice and look at the brightness of the star group of Pleiades, we have Makemake again and maybe he brings another chance for us to learn his ways.

To finish this chapter I must return once more to the words of the crewmember who sailed on the recent historic voyage to Easter Island on a re-constructed twin hulled ocean-going canoe using only sails, stars and the sea.

> "Surrounded by an immense sea and forced to turn inward, we had discovered a harmony within ourselves and with the natural world. For all of us, this voyage had been a rare gift of mana."

These are touching words. We must listen to Makemake again.

> "…..the traveler….is struck by the solemnity and picturesque beauty of the scene, and is led to ponder on the strange law of progress, which looks so like retrogression, and which in so many distant parts of the world has exterminated or driven out a highly artistic and constructive race, to make room for one which, as far as we can judge is very far it's inferior."

William Thomson, Paymaster of the U.S.S. Mohican, 1891.

Illustration 17. *The beautiful land of Hawaii that is Haumea*

HAUMEA, GODDESS OF HAWAII, BIRTH, NATURE, ROCK AND FIRE

Haumea the Dwarf Planet and the Dispute in Which Two Men Claimed Her.

The circumstances surrounding a planet`s discovery tell us a lot about the meaning of that planet in astrology and the meaning of the planet Haumea was beautifully obvious right from the beginning of her emergence into the collective consciousness of the 21st century. The planet Haumea announced herself with the brightest of light and a discovery story involving 2 groups of men (astronomers) both claiming her as their own and thus revealing some of her meaning

Haumea the planet was discovered by the astronomer Mike Brown around Christmas of 2004. He gave her the nickname `Santa` and began making the detailed observations necessary. He should really have announced her to the world in July 2005, but he had to take paternity leave instead.

In July 2005 by a team of Spanish astronomers headed by Jose-Luis Ortiz also claimed discovery of Haumea. They were examining data collected in 2003 when they had their Eureka moment, but unlike the Mike Brown team, they made a few quick enquiries and quickly registered their claim with the official committee. This meant the discovery was technically theirs. Unfortunately the `quick enquires` had meant they accessed the publicly available web logs of the Mike Brown team. Mike then accused them of stealing his data with no previous awareness of Haumea; an accusation the Ortiz team denies.

Because the official naming department couldn`t sort this out, they decided eventually to say that Haumea had been discovered in Spain but declined to give anyone`s name as official discoverer. So no one man could claim her as his own. Both the American and the Spanish teams had suggested names for her, but the Spanish choice had to be discounted because they had chosen a Spanish Underworld goddess and Underworld names could only be linked to a different part of the solar system. The naming department must have been relieved because this meant they could go with the American name. The guy in charge of this committee said the controversy was the worst in 400 years.[1] This same chap also expressed amazement that Haumea hadn`t been found before[2] and this is where I say it was always going to happen like this. Behold the mystery of astrology! Haumea was so bright she could be seen with even a junior telescope. Why is it that all those astronomers in all those centuries didn`t spot her and then two discover her at the same time? Isn`t it funny how planets can`t be seen until the time is right and then they emerge to tell us something about coming change on planet Earth. Haumea chose the circumstances and the year of her discovery, Mike Brown and Jose-Luiz Ortiz were simply pawns in her game.

Why the Name Haumea Was Chosen

Haumea has two moons that were discovered in 2005 using a big telescope on Hawaii and it was during this time that the name was chosen by David Rabinowitz of the American team.[3] The planet was known to be made of solid rock and the Hawaiian goddess of that name has close associations with stone. It was also recognised that the planet had been hit by something big that had knocked lumps of rocky ice from her body. These surround her orbit and two of them are even large enough to be moons. In Hawaiian myth Haumea is the mother of many other deities that are formed from pieces of her body.

Haumea is also the Hawaiian goddess of childbirth and Mike Brown was prevented from announcing Haumea`s discovery because his wife went into labour and gave birth to their daughter. These things by themselves make the choice of name appropriate, but there was significantly and coincidently much more to come!

President Obama and a Hawaiian Planet

When the suggestion was put forward for the name Haumea, no one could have dreamed that 2 years later, just as the name was finally being announced, a young mixed race senator would run for the office of President of the United States of America and win. President Barack Obama was born in Hawaii. Astrology needed to symbolise the changes that happen when the world`s most important superpower changes it`s leader, so sure enough the strange hand of fate worked it`s magic. Synchronous with the arrival of a Hawaiian president was the arrival of a Hawaiian planet!

Peculiar Features of the Planet

Haumea is the strangest object found to date in the solar system. She is shaped like a cigar and actually spins end over end, completing a full circuit in just 4 hours. Another strange feature is a red spot on her icy surface.[4]

In 2008 scientists were reporting that they had found 8 parts of the planet scattered around the Kuiper belt. These are remarkable because they are so shiny. This is even more remarkable when we consider that there are 8 main islands of Hawaii, and in myth Haumea produces 8 offspring which are formed out of her own body.

Haumea, the Goddess of Hawaiian Mythology

Haumea has several different guises, all to do with creating or giving birth. In one she is a human, confusingly called `Papa` and married to a guy called Wakea. She is thought to be the first woman on Hawaii and therefore original mother and ancestor to the royal family who always inter-bred to maintain their pure bloodline. According to Beckworth, she is also the feminine principle or goddess who creates the islands of Hawaii. The 8 islands are all volcanoes that run along a fault line; some of which still erupt. When they do the lava spews out, then cools and adds to the landmass. The fire within the volcano is Haumea in her Fire goddess form called Pele.

The old Hawaiians have watched the process of land being formed from volcanoes and it has provided them with a wonderful metaphor or model for understanding how the Earth was created. They equate the fire with Spirit, which is exactly right in spiritual terms, and see that Earth is formed out of Fire. The old Islanders said that the Islands rose up as the body of Spirit. They were the material form of spiritual force……. and this means that land has an animate nature.[5]

Hawaiian Creation Chant

The Hawaiians did not write to record their history, it was told in chants which were learnt more seriously than the western world learns it`s nursery rhymes. They had an important one called the Creation chant, which has many different versions on the 8 main islands. One striking feature is how well they all describe evolution from slime and tiny sea creatures through to larger marine life and mammals. A translation by the last Hawaiian Queen in 1897 says, "Curious students will notice in this chant, analogies between its accounts of the creation and that given by modern science or sacred scripture."[6] She also made the point that "The ancient Hawaiians were astronomers, and the terms used appertained to the heavens, the stars, terrestrial science, and the gods." The chant is very long but basically says that the primordial soup was readied and then came `Time` which supported the Earth and held the Heavens. There is much reference to Yin (feminine) and Yang (masculine) energies producing all manner of things living and the god/dessess or spirit which pre-exist mankind and are brought into being in their earthly guises - such as surf, octopuses, strife, boils and deep holes. The Hawaiians believe that sacred spirit or deity exists in all things.

Haumea is called different names from Lailai to Papa showing that she can take on many different guises; morphing from old woman to young girl and becoming her own daughter or granddaughter. We are told that as Haumea, she is great and fearless and has 8 different forms ranging from a shark to a goddess or spirit and a human woman. Haumea gave birth to children from her brain amidst slime and they would become chiefs, islands or human babies. So to put it in a nutshell she is Mother Nature transformed into anything. There are long lists of things that are yin or feminine in nature, or yang and masculine.

Haumea as Goddess of Fertility in Wild Plants and Forest

In one particular Island myth we are told that Haumea`s priestesses were privileged to be given a supply of wild food when famine befell the rest of the land. The implication here is that if we are sufficiently knowledgeable about the food that nature naturally supplies then we will be able to eat when mass produced agriculture fails. In another myth a net thrown over her kills Haumea and this same net is used during a Makahiki festival, which shakes food over the land to encourage good crops. The meaning being that wild food and plants are killed to grow farmed foods. The guy who throws the net over Haumea is called Kaulu, whose name means `growth in plants`. Myth says that he withdraws crops from the land and for some reason this forces Haumea to produce wild food because the soil will not just remain barren; one of god/desses has to provide. Apparently Haumea had wanted to vent her anger by withholding her wild food but it must be provided when cultivated crops are not available at certain time of the year. This shows that although Haumea is destroyer and guardian of wild growth she can be killed by being `netted` or controlled and will have to succumb to some conditions.[7]

However Haumea`s myths aren`t always about wild food. In some she possessed a magic stick called Makalei that could attract seafood and was associated with a tree of never-failing food supply.[8]

Haumea as Goddess of Childbirth and Fire

The Hawaiians were told through myth that Haumea could secure a painless childbirth. She was also talked of in the Hawaiian Book of Medicine as being able to prevent a Caesarean birth. She would use chants, incantations and herbal medicine to procure a natural birth. Haumea herself was continually growing old and then being re-born and this could describe the process whereby the volcanic islands of the Pacific are born, sink into the sea and then new ones rise up again. As the volcanoes gave birth so easily, so Haumea could make this happen for humans. Haumea was the whole world to them in one form or another and in fact, all the myths describe Haumea as being and doing everything that their island home does.

One or two myths call her the goddess of underground heat. This alludes to the red heat inside the Earth that spills from the volcanoes and the contents of the uterus. It is said in one myth that the fire goddess Pele was born from between Haumea`s thighs. Others in the Pele family were born from parts of Haumea`s body. Pele was the goddess who lived in volcanoes and sent floods of lava to burn everything; she was said to influence those whose lives were filled with burning anger against their fellow men. Pele was in constant combat with one of her sisters, the ocean. Another sister, Hiʻiaka, was a cherished favourite and born in the shape of an egg.

The Layers of the Multiverse Compared to Hawaiian Culture

The Hawaiian culture and history is deeply suggestive of hierarchy and `layers` of significance. Their verbal mythology, handed from Clan Chief to Clan Chief in the form of sacred chants, contains long lists of who-begat-who with emphasis on sacred incestuous lineage. They had a heavily demarcated class system of servant families, commoners, upper class and royalty. They had a sacred Creation chant that talked of clearly defined `Eras` and their spiritual understanding of the other realms included dimensions of sky gods, earthly spirits and mischief makers, household gods, the home of the spirits of the ancestors and finally the Underworld. Haumea herself had several rebirths, reappearing as her own daughter and then granddaughter; each time marrying her son-in-law and grand-son-in-law.

What Does Haumea Represent in the 21st Century?

Unlike Sedna and Makemake, whose meanings have been obvious from the word go, Haumea is taking her time to come out of the closet. Apart from the obvious so far and her synchronicity with the arrival of a Hawaiian president, she kept fairly quiet in the first decade of the 21st century. She may well represent women's issues and maybe even those of minority groups, such as homosexual men. There are also some early associations with evolution such as baby dinosaur skeletons, but at the time of writing it is too early to tell. This chapter then, is necessarily short since her story is not ready to be told. We do know the following, however.

Haumea Rules Natural Cycles Such as Those of the Moon

The ancient Hawaiian indigenous people hallowed the Moon and the lunar cycle was of paramount importance for planting and harvesting. Every day of the cycle had a different meaning with associated instructions and this was ruled over by the aristocracy and the sacred laws of taboo. Each Hawaiian knew exactly where the Moon was on that day and just what that meant. According to Clive Ruggles, the importance placed on the position of the Moon and agriculture is still practised today.[9]

The weight of the Moon and it`s gravity is so strong that as it passes over the surface of the Earth all the water in the oceans is pulled towards it in big hump. Even the Earth`s crust and core is pulled out of alignment by 5% as the Moon passes overhead on her 29-ish day journey around it. This cycle and rhythm is fundamental to our existence and spiritual well-being and yet we have all tuned it out and tuned in to street lamps, microwaves and mobile phone masts. Hopefully, Haumea`s arrival will mean that the old Hawaiian ways are going to be important in the coming century and we will learn to live that way again.

In the Hawaiian chant we are told that her fabled husband Wakea, became `false` to her and out of jealousy tried to re-order the natural rhythms she had established; moving the Moon`s days around and using taboo to stop her crossing her threshold.[10] This is a nice metaphor for how humans and science try to control Mother Nature. However, just as her discovery by two astronomy teams at the same time meant that none could claim her, so the human race may find that they cannot claim, own or control her either.

Circadian Rhythms and Breast Cancer

Scientific research[11] was published in 2009, to support the theory that un-natural light at un-natural times causes various forms of cancer. Haumea's natural rhythms of night and day, darkness and light are severely disrupted by the 24 hour working of industrialised nations. Especially at risk are women night workers, who are exposed to a greater risk of breast cancer. This alarming fact is even more astonishing when comparisons are made to blind female night workers, who are getting *less* breast cancer. Apparently, breast tumors are awake during the daylight hours, but rest during the night because the melatonin produced by the body in the dark, puts them to sleep. This inactive period dulls the disease because the human, nocturnal, circadian, melatonin signal inhibits human breast cancer growth. Circadian rhythms are physical, mental, and behavioral changes that occur in living things and follow a 24-hour cycle, responding primarily to light and darkness in the environment. Apparently, there are abnormally low cancer incidence rates in regions where there is no light for economic reasons. Perhaps candle light would be more appropriate than white strip lights which seem to do most damage.

In astrology there is an association between the Moon and the breasts, so this is a very interesting in the light of the myth regarding Haumea's fabled husband and his meddling with her natural rhythms and Moon days.

Hawaiian Spiritual Concept Has Now Been Proven Scientifically

As I have already stated several times in different chapters, science has now proven that all matter is made up of energetic force that whizzes so fast it seems solid. This force pervades and exists in all things giving them dynamic life or energy. It is mysterious and they call it `dark`. In spiritual understanding this energetic force is that of the element of Fire. This element holds spirit, deity, gnosis and what we understand to be god/desses or the Holy Spirit.

The Hawaiian`s have always expressed this belief through their mythology but also through the way they lived their lives. They had abject, absolute, unquestioning conviction and faith in this as the meaning of life. In the same way that their volcanic islands arose out of the sea from the fire at the centre of the Earth, the material body is formed out of `spirit` or energy.

This has to be why Haumea has emerged into world consciousness. Her astrological meaning points out the synchronicity between Polynesian spiritual beliefs and the new understanding of fundamental existence that science is rapidly achieving.

> "Behind the (Papa and Wakea legend) is the Polynesian mythical conception of a dark formless spirit world presided over by the female element, and a world of form born out of the spirit world and to which it again returns, made visible and active in this human life through light as the impregnating male element."[12]

That single sentence is actually breathtaking in it`s absolute accuracy of the New World scientific and spiritual vision of 2008. However, it was written in 1940!

Haumea as Nature and Sacred Earth

It is difficult for us in western culture to even begin to understand the Hawaiian spiritual concept. And yet it more accurately reflects the true composition and nature of life on Earth and in the Cosmos than our monotheist (one god) separatist culture does.

An Hawaiian cultural historian says this:

> "Hawaiian culture evolved in close partnership with it`s natural environment. Thus Hawaiian culture does not have a clear dividing line of where culture ends and nature begins. In a traditional Hawaiian context, nature and culture are one and the same, there is no division between the two."[13]

They had such a healthy relationship with their land and nature they themselves were healthy and so was their land. In the West we are either poisoning our land, or piling concrete on it. We intensively rear poor chickens so that thousands are crammed into appalling conditions with no space or light. They are so weak they cannot even stand up and they have no feathers from stress and crouching in their own excreta. Supermarkets proudly sell their bodies for £2.

We don`t understand that what we do to chickens and our land affects our spiritual well being because we are all part of the same Universal Spirit or Force; it is part of us and it exists in all things. The force, energy and spirit of Mother Nature or Haumea IS the landscape and it also us. I think this is something we will all have to learn……one way or another.

"Behind (the Haumea legend) is a Polynesian mythical conception of a dark formless spirit world presided over by the female element, and a world of form born out of the spirit world and to which it again returns….."

BECKWORTH, M. Hawaiian Mythology pp306. (1940)

CHAPTER 8

Illustration 18. *The fiery Eris.*

ERIS, GODDESS OF STRIFE, STIMULATION & RIVALRY

After spending the last two chapters in Polynesia and the Pacific Ocean, we now return once more to ancient Greece. But this time, instead of grappling with concepts of separate dimensions and our creation and place in the Multiverse, we are lectured on personal responsibility and the laws of natural justice. Like Ceres, Eris is within our personal grasp and although mighty in her effect, we *can* learn to respect and work with her.

The Discovery of Eris, Thought to be the Tenth Planet

Eris is in the Kuiper belt, the doughnut shaped ring of planets, rocks and icy debris around the very edge of our Solar System. She was discovered along with Haumea, Makemake and Sedna by Mike Brown and his team during a 5 year survey that took place early in the 21st century. Eris was first photographed in October 2003, but it takes them a while to sift through all these photographs, so it wasn`t until January 2005 that an ecstatic Mike Brown realised he had a big planet on his hands and unofficially called the planet Xena and her moon Gabrielle. The nickname Xena had been taken from the hit television series `Xena the Warrior Princess`, and the name Gabrielle from her sidekick in the show.

Eris is actually bigger than Pluto and was therefore entitled to be called the 10th planet, so the discovery was earth shattering.... but then came the problems! If you remember back to the chapter on Haumea, two separate teams of astronomers discovered her at a similar time and this started a squabble for ownership. One of Mike Brown`s main concerns was that the other Spanish team was calling Haumea the 10th planet, which Mike Brown knew to be untrue because he had the much bigger Eris up his sleeve. In an effort to make sure that Eris got her rightful recognition as the biggest, he hastily called a press conference and announced Eris to the world in July 2005, which was before they had planned to do so. Mike Brown was angry with the Spanish team and described them as "hackers" without "scruples".[1] I should imagine the Jose Luiz-Ortiz team weren`t very impressed with this. Then an international row erupted about the term `planet`, and this had to be decided before Eris could be properly named. The international astronomers held a "raucous" meeting that made new rules and stopped Eris being named the 10th planet of the Solar System. These new rules meant that Pluto would no longer be called the 9th planet of the Solar System and was demoted to `dwarf planet` status along with Eris. All that took an awful lot of meeting and rule-making, so it wasn`t until September of 2006 that Xena and her moon Gabrielle were finally given the official names of Eris and Dysnomia.

There is an interesting coincidence here. Dysnomia is the daughter of Eris in myth. Dysnomia is the Greek goddess of lawlessness, and in the show `Xena the Warrior Princess`, the part of Xena is played by Lucy Lawless – her real married name!

Another interesting coincidence is provided by the horoscope of Lucy Lawless, which features a very strong connection to this planet. It says that the destiny and purpose of her whole life will be firmly bound up with the energies of the planet Xena/Eris. Lucy is quoted the Universal Studios show literature as saying that she loves "being as psycho as I can possibly be." (For the astrology buffs -Eris con juncts Sun, Moon, Asc. N.N. and Saturn in Aries in the 1st house of Lucy`s natal chart.)

The write up of the show speaks volumes:

> "In a time of ancient gods, warlords and kings, a mighty princess is forged in the heat of battle. Her name is Xena, and only her courage and passion can restore order to a world in turmoil, a world crying out for a hero!"[2]

Those are extremely comforting words in this day and age. Could Eris really be our hero? The mythology reported by her discoverers is as follows:

> "In Greek mythology, Eris is the goddess of discord and strife. She stirs up jealousy and envy to cause fighting and anger amongst men. All the gods were invited to a wedding with the exception of Eris. Enraged at her exclusion, she spitefully caused a quarrel among the goddesses that led to the Trojan War."[3]

At first glance, it is hard to see a similarity between these two descriptions but we`ll press on!

Although dwarf planet Eris is usually much further out than Pluto, and takes about 560 years to go round our Sun, she has an egg shaped orbit and sometimes comes slightly closer to the Sun than Pluto. At the moment she is the farthest out she gets, at 97 times the distance between the Sun and the Earth.[4] She will be at her closest in 2257, when she will be 38 times the distance between the Sun and the Earth. Her brightness is surprising her discoverers though, so even though she is so far away, her influence cannot be ignored. She has been in the Zodiac sign of Aries since her discovery and will not leave this sign until around the middle of the 21st century. You will particularly feel her influence if you are were born on, or shortly after 9th April.

A Religious Cult Called Discordianism

When the Romans adopted Eris they called her Discordia, and she is often referred to as the goddess of chaos. Strangely, in 1958/9 a cult religion was formed (supposedly in a bowling ally!), which adopted the theme of discord and chaos and called itself Discordianism. It`s proponents recognise that disharmony and chaos are valid aspects of reality, and have a real place in the universe. They offer an alternative to organised religion, which they see as the "opium of the masses". Since the naming of Eris, this group has had an upsurge in popularity, with Amazon selling out of their original books. (This will be astrologers trying to find out what the planet means!)

The Mythology of Eris

According to Greek mythology, Eris is the goddess of strife and when the Romans adopted her they called her Discordia. She is either the sister or the companion of the god of war, Ares. We are told that the Greek Eris is sinister and mean, and her greatest joy is to make trouble. When she was not invited to a prominent wedding, she turned up with a golden apple with the words "for the fairest" inscribed on it, and tossed this before the group of the most important goddesses. This being Hera, the wife of Zeus; Athena, a warrior goddess and Aphrodite, the goddess of love, beauty and sex. The goddesses obviously began quarrelling with one another over who was the most beautiful and they eventually called on the king of gods, Zeus to choose between them. Recognising the trouble that would befall if him if did, he ordered a mortal man called Paris to choose a winner from the 3 of them. Paris chose Aphrodite after she promised to make the most beautiful woman in the world fall in love with him. This happened to be Helen of Troy who was already married, and the consequential love affair started the Trojan War.

In the Dictionary of Classical Antiquities[5] we are told that Eris is the goddess of discord, fighting and quarrelling. Further snippets about her tell us that she calls forth war and according to the Iliad she wanders about small and insignificant at first, but she soon raises her head up to heaven.

Her Other Associations in Myth

Eris is the daughter of night and mother of such god/desses or things as trouble, toil, oblivion, hunger, pain, murder, carnage, brawls, disputes, ruin, forgetfulness, deceit and finally lawlessness.[6] (Never did a goddess look so attractive!) Here you see how the ancient Greeks, just like the early Polynesians, believed that the god/dessess *were* the feelings and energies of living; the natural responses of human beings and civilisation. The gods were not separate individuals; they could be parts of the personality or the archetypal feelings and responses that we all experience. So we each have the potential to unleash our Eris and then encounter the difficulties or god/desses that she gave birth to. For instance you could experience the feeling that you have not been acknowledged for something you feel proud of, and this would stir the revengeful Eris in you. Feeling snubbed and humiliated you might then experience carnage, brawls, disputes and ruin, or any other of the god/desses that Eris gave birth to. Mythology was used to counsel the population on a simple level and introduce them to life`s lessons.

A Goddess Who Represents the Natural Law of Fire and the Chaos of the Godness

All the religions and sacred texts of the world have a creation myth with an orderly universe being created out of chaos, Fire, energy and spirit. This realm is the 96% of the Multiverse and everything in our Universe draws from it. In this quantum realm, particles that make up an atom are very `excited` vortices of energy that move at light speed and beyond. Eris is a representative of this realm of Fire. In myth, she so delights in the tumult of war, she stays on the battlefield rejoicing in the havoc when the other gods have withdrawn. It is this movement and excitability that is Eris`s delight; the chaos is exhilarating and she feels elation in the mayhem.

The Positive Side of Eris in Myth

But there is a more positive side to Eris. In the myth, she only caused trouble because she was not being included. Her story seems to say that she is clever, and if we exclude her, she will find a way to make her energy felt. Her discovery included a squabble between the world`s top astronomer; but it forced them to sort out some things that had been ignored for years. Namely, their computer security, `new planet` protocol and Pluto`s true status. This all needed doing.

According to the Dictionary of Classical Antiquities, "She was the personification of noble rivalry, and is represented as stimulating even dullards to exertion."[7] However, as we shall now see, the Greek writer Hesiod had the greatest insights into the positive aspects of Eris.

Using Hesiod to Understand How to Engage With Eris Energy in The Most Positive Way

Living Life to Take Advantage of Eris`s Competitiveness

In order for Eris energy to be effective it is naturally very strong, volatile and vicious. The energy can easily become "slanderous-tongued Envy, with look of deadly hate, rejoicing in the misfortunes of others."[8]

However, in all my work and in all my days, I have always found that there is a positive side to everything, including misfortune, and Eris is no different. I was therefore pleased to find an excellent dissertation written by a Heber Michel Hayes in 1918 for the University of Chicago, and I refer to it here. This dissertation is an examination of a piece of writing by the Greek philosopher Hesiod called "The Works and Days" and arguably written in the 6th to 8th century.[9]

There is a good and bad Eris and the whole energy is essentially about ethics and karma. The bad Eris is "lawless strife" which has no regard for others and is often demonstrated by the animal kingdom, whilst the good Eris energy abides by natural justice and is stirred into serious and purposeful action.

In order to get the best out of this powerful goddess, mortals are urged to stop their emotions (that is – their other god/desses) being swayed by Eris`s cruel and spiteful passions. We should also avoid not caring for others, cruel recklessness and wickedness or perversity. But most of all there are two things required of mortals and these are labour and justice. Let`s have a look at the labour part first. Perses is urged to stop bad Eris taking him into vengeful acts that will prevent him labouring and Hay`s interpretation of Hesiod explains this in the following way.

Good Eris will support the worker who passes another worker in the race for wealth and prosperity. This worker should not make attempts to get other people`s stuff dishonestly, but should work with honest labour to attain excellence and the highest goal. The good Eris is a blessing because she gives us a healthy envy of others that will stir us into action when we see their achievements. We look at their wealth and industry and determine to achieve our own success. If we go with the bad Eris then we may get involved in vengeful acts of envy that waste our time and prevent our own success. Hesiod clearly demonstrates the two different faces of Eris and Hays says:

> "They are vividly portrayed, the one impelling to dishonest and forcible aggression, the other to honorable and peaceful competition. The dramatic opposition of the two is striking."

Hesiod`s demonstration of the two different aspects of Eris once again brings up the duality or two-sides theme of the Kuiper Belt planets. Things are never what they seem on the surface.

Good Eris As Part Of The Natural System of Justice.

Eris gave birth to energy that will punish perjurers or those who don`t honour their oaths. She will see to it that those who lie to win are punished.

We are especially warned against legal trials in an effort to extract that which is not morally ours. Since the western culture is entranced with `no win, no fee` solicitors and loves suing or blaming others for misfortune, then I think Eris`s emergence is nicely timed. Solicitors beware.

In an effort to get the right balance we should hang on to and develop our scruples (the god Aidos) and our indignation at wrong doing (the god Nemesis), keeping a healthy balance between the two. Eris has a family who are personifications of human and karmic ethics, many of which can be found in the Polynesian social system of taboo and mana that we looked at in the Makemake chapter. It is obvious that she is heavily implicated in a divinely instigated and policed moral system of repercussions and encouragement.

Hesiod declared that we can profit from Eris energy by accepting the laws of Zeus and not bribing the judges to win. The Greeks had avenging spirits called the Erinyes who sorted out retributive justice and they were responsible for punishing crimes not within the reach of human justice[10] and satisfying Oath who is born of Eris. Apparently Oath does more damage than any other to mortals when they knowingly swear to a falsehood. We should trust in the divine providence of Zeus, which means trust that the spirit and divinity of the 96% will attend to things and we should not enter into ruinous strife trying to sort it ourselves. (Ok, sounds fine to me!)

Some Final Thoughts On Eris

Eris energy has a way of making us feel that we have been got at or picked on, and perhaps this is what earned her such a bad reputation in early Greece. Myth tells us that she `loves increasing the moaning of men`, and there is no doubt that Eris can indeed produce some very irritating energy! On the day that you get overheard by the boss as you call him terrible names on the phone……or you get zapped by a speed trap….. or your computer gets an unlockable virus…..you can be sure that Eris is sticking an oar in. But hey!…perhaps you should have left the job years ago….or shouldn`t have been speeding….. or should have updated your virus software! Most especially, it seems, we should not engage in bitterness and vitriol when it appears that life or someone else has gotten the better of us. We do get some very encouraging philosophy from Hesiod on her useful aspects and thanks to this we can understand and perhaps trust and follow the good Eris. That is our choice. We can use her energy to labour hard and surpass others with our industry, or we can wallow in spiteful jealousy and moaning.

We are told in myth that she wanders around small and insignificant to start with, but soon raises her head. It is apparent that she is still in the `small and insignificant` phase, and we haven`t really seen the extent of what Eris can do yet. Mike Brown is convinced that she has the power to start world war 3, and although he is not an astrologer, he has experienced Eris's very potent energy for himself. However, I would like to go back to the words of the publicity men in Xena, the Warrior Princess:

> "A mighty princess is forged in the heat of battle and only her courage and passion can restore order to a world in turmoil, a world crying out for a hero."

Planet Earth is in a mess right now, so maybe we need a goddess who will stir us into serious labour and purposeful action. This could be a good time to invite her to the party.........we know what will happen if we don`t!

Chapter 9

Illustration 19 *Sedna within her sea creatures of the Artic*

SEDNA, THE PRIDE AND OUTRAGE OF THE GREAT OCEAN GODDESS

And now we near the end of our journey of discovery. We don't near the end of our learning, for that has only just begun, but we near the end of our introduction to that which will become familiar. The last leg of our journey takes us to the Northern-most inhabited lands of planet Earth, to the Inuit or Eskimo people of Greenland and Canada and their Sea goddess Sedna.

Sedna, a Strange New Planet.

Sedna was discovered in 2003 by Mike Brown, Chad Trujillo and David Rabinowitz; the same team that discovered Eris, Haumea and Makemake during the QUEST survey. Her name was announced to the world in 2004, but….the discoverers have yet to decide *what* she is. This strange and unusual object is so alien to our known universe physically, that her discoverers and world-class scientists were speechless, confused and baffled when they found her. Sedna is very, very far away and there is nothing else like her. Planets near to Earth and the Sun take around a year or two to make one complete circle of the Sun. Sedna has a very strange orbit that takes over 10,500 years to complete.[1] She swings out in a great oval shaped loop which extends right out into space before swinging back in again. No-one knows why she does this, but there is an intriguing theory that it could be because there is something big out there that we haven't discovered yet and it's gravity knocks her off course.[2] The Kuiper belt just stops dead on it's outer edge; it doesn't peter out slowly, so there is speculation that this is because a big planet gobbled up all the little ones.

When Sedna is the furthest away she is 83,700,000,000 miles from the Sun. That's 84 billion miles. And even when she is in the part of her loop that is nearest to us, she is still 3 times further out than Pluto[3], and that's still an unimaginably long way! Our Sun would look so small from Sedna, that if you were to stand on her surface and hold up a pin, you could hide the Sun behind the head of the pin.

There is a theory that, half way to the next star there is a cloud of bits and pieces called the Oort cloud. The theory goes that every so often comets break away from this and travel inwards towards our Sun and there is speculation that Sedna might have come from that cloud. However it is all so far away it is undetectable. For us to be able to detect something, it has to emit heat or reflect light and then our instruments can see it. The stars, for instance, emit light so they can be seen. Planets close enough to the Sun can be seen because they reflect the Sun's light and heat. But rocks or planets that are too far from our Sun to reflect the light cannot be picked up. Sedna was just close enough and just shiny enough to reflect a tiny bit of our Sun's light, but the Oort cloud, if it exists, is even further out than Sedna. It is estimated that her surface temperature is a chilly minus 400° Fahrenheit and this prompted Mike Brown to pick a goddess from the indigenous population of the Arctic Circle for her name.

It was quickly recognised that we would need an expanding vocabulary of classifications or labels, so we would know what to call new space objects; particularly unusual ones, like Sedna (planet, asteroid, comet etc.). So the world's astronomers got together in August 2006 and after much debate came up with the term…….. ……..object! Yes, object! So Sedna is an `object`. (An Inner Oort cloud Object to give her the full title.) But that doesn't seem appropriate for such a special entity and some astronomers are calling her a `planetoid`. Obviously I am including her in a book about dwarf planets and this is mainly because she was discovered in the same survey by the same team and so has as much to say about our future as the rest of the dwarf planets. However, the description of dwarf planet is technically wrong. Just to make it easy I'm going to use the term `planetoid` because I think she deserves some status, and she doesn't seem to be the kind of goddess we should sniff at, as you will read!

As with Pluto, size definitely does not count. Sedna is about half the size of our Moon, and yet she has been powerful enough to cause all kinds of weather events here on Earth.

The Myth of Sedna

The planetoid Sedna is named after a Goddess of the Inuit or `Eskimo` tribes who live in northern Canada and Greenland. Her discoverers compared her isolation in the icy, cold, distant reaches of our Solar System with the bottom of the frigid sea in the icy, distant reaches of the Arctic[3]. As they usually picked the names of Greek or Roman deities, this was an unusual departure from normal practice. But Sedna had broken all the nice neat rules of the solar system model with her very existence, so why not break a few more? And that choice of name has turned out to be stunningly appropriate. After only a few years of observation, Sedna the planetoid is clearly representing the themes of her myth, and astrological prediction involving her is not difficult. The worldwide storms and floods of 2006-08 were easy to predict, for instance.

Myths are stories that demonstrate the issues that are important for that culture. Northern Canada and Greenland are vast areas and their cultural, environmental and survival needs alter according to their local issues. This probably explains why there are so many different versions of her myth. This particular one was published by the anthropologist Franz Boas in 1888.[4]

Sedna was raised by her father and grew up to be a very beautiful girl. Many suitors came to ask for her hand in marriage, but she was proud and considered none of them good enough. Then one day a bird called a fulmar (related to the albatross) arrived and coaxed Sedna with an offer she couldn't refuse. "Come into the land of the birds, where there is never hunger, where my tent is made of the most beautiful skins. You shall rest on soft bearskins. My fellows, the fulmars, shall bring you all your heart may desire; their feathers shall clothe you; your lamp shall always be filled with oil, your pot with meat." Suitably impressed, Sedna agreed, and they set out on the long journey to his homeland. Sedna then discovered that her new husband had lied and her new home was freezing-cold hard rock, with a few fish skins and feathers. Her bed was hard and she had to live on raw fish, which the birds brought her. The myth makes the point that her pride had made her reject the Inuit youth. She cried in the wind to her father, saying that the birds treated her unkindly and she felt like a stranger and wanted to return home. Her father eventually arrived, and hearing of her plight agreed to take her home. He killed the fulmar, and set off with Sedna in his boat for home. When the other fulmars found their companion dead and his wife gone, they flew after them. (The story goes that they were very sad over the death of their poor murdered comrade and this explains their mournful cries until this day.)

They found Sedna and father and stirred up a raging storm. The sea rose in immense waves that threatened the pair with destruction. Fearing for his life, the father offered Sedna to the birds by flinging her overboard, but she clung to the edge of the boat. The cruel father then took a knife and cut off the first joints of her fingers. Falling into the sea they were transformed into whales, the nails turning into whalebone. Sedna still clung to the boat, so he cut off her second finger joints, which swam away as seals, and when the father finally cut off the stumps of the fingers they became ground seals.

This version reports that Sedna was finally allowed back into the boat by her father, but life was still very unpleasant after that. Other versions say that after her father cut off her fingers, she sank to the bottom of the ocean and became the supreme ocean goddess.

There are some wildly different stories, but her early refusal to marry seems consistent. The Inuits seem to make the point that she didn't come from them, and she wouldn't marry into them. Another consistent story line throughout all the different myths is that her fingers are cut off, and these become sea creatures.

What Does Sedna's Myth Mean To the Inuit People

This myth is a wonderful metaphor for Man, the patriarchal or masculine, versus Mother Nature, the matriarchal or feminine. It shows how man has treated Mother Nature. How we have abused her for our own ends and how she has tried to be creative even when repeatedly attacked. For instance, when her fingers were cut off she turned them into beautiful seals and walruses. The myth explains the outrage and fury that Sedna now turns on Man and the patriarchal. It explains in simple terms how Man will strive to control Mother Nature but how she will always win in the end. Sedna is the most important and dominant of Inuit deities. She controls the supply of seafood and if she doesn't play ball, the Inuit people starve.

Sedna and the Shaman

As Goddess of the Oceans, Sedna applies strict rules and conditions for the Inuit to fish by, or she withholds the seas bounty until properly appeased. One of these strict rules is with regard to the animal as it is killed. The hunter must not damage[5] or injure the animal and then leave it in pain, he must properly kill it. If any rule is broken, or the animal wasn't properly respected, the tribe's shaman leader, called an angekkok, has to appease her by making a spiritual or shamanic journey to visit her in the Inuit underworld. This introduces us to the concept of the shaman and shamanic practise, which may be on the rise in Western spiritual circles. The angekkok will face a series of obstacles as he makes his way down to Adlivun,[6] the kingdom of Sedna. He may meet a dog (some myths say her husband was a dog, not a fulmar) or Sedna's father who will attempt to attack the shaman. When he finally reaches Sedna he must comb her hair whilst finding out what the tribe must put right before they starve. Obviously she doesn't have the fingers to comb her own hair and apparently the evil deeds of humans are like dirt in her hair, so the shaman has to comb them out. The manner is which the angekkok engages with Sedna exposes one of the effects that Sedna can have on people personally; he can either be aggressive and violent, or submissive and serving. He may even repeat the process of cutting off her fingers to release the sea creatures that will feed the human population.

Inuit shamans have spiritual powers that enable them to pass into a coma or state of trance. He is said to taken over by spirit and he may shout scream and struggle in seizure. He may also speak in ancient dialects or be physically sick. When he comes round again, he will tell of future weather conditions and expected fishing or hunting success.

Primal Force of Nature and Stroppy Red Head

Sedna is believed to be one of the primal forces of nature by the Inuit people. She is both deeply feared and deeply respected. From her position as Goddess of the sea, Sedna now controls the ultimate power over the survival of the whole Inuit race, and appears quite demanding and stroppy with it. The Inuits also have a moon-god who has powers over water but he is less ferocious. After first being abused by the males in her life, Sedna then becomes powerful and abusive back. Her fury can be seen in the power of the storms she sends, which will now make man now pay homage to her. The Shaman may comb her hair as an act of humbleness and reverence. This tells of her vanity and her pride, but also points to her wounding at the hands of the patriarchy and how he must tend to her as a result of her wound. She cannot tend to her self, but she demands this act of subservience as repayment.

It is interesting that Sedna the `planet` or `object` has a reddish tinge to her light, which is puzzling the scientists. In the myth Sedna was initially renowned for her pride and her refusal to submit to several suitors. It seems she has the character of the archetypal redhead, although her hair is said to be black.

Animals and Humans are Interchangeable

The story mixes together human and animal figures, meaning we are almost interchangeable. Their beliefs really support the common esoteric principle that we are all one energy or unity but with different forces of nature to keep in balance. Sedna is seen as a creative and destructive all pervading presence.

In his article `The Animal and the Human`, Malcolm Kenton has this to say:

> "A central aspect of the religious traditions of several Eskimo tribes … is the existence of the Sea Mother, who is both as a real creature living on the ocean floor and a spirit residing within sea creatures (as well as land creatures, according to some tribes)…….
>
> Since the Eskimo depend on sea creatures for most of their food supply, keeping the Sea Mother happy is an important aspect of their endeavours. She is seen as having control of the souls of many creatures, which are able to take either animal or human form, and as a union of opposites. Her power is respected as greater than the human because people are utterly dependent on other creatures for survival."[7]

What Does Sedna Mean Now

Naming a planetoid after Sedna signifies an enormous awakening of her energy and meaning in the Collective. This boosts the divine feminine energy in the Cosmos with a prominent and controlling symbol of outrage, pride and nobility, but Sedna also has some other specific associations. As with all the planets or god/desses, where it is possible, they can symbolise abundance *or* depletion of these associations. For instance, Sedna represents the frozen polar regions and these are disappearing fast. She also represents animals that depend on the icy conditions, such as polar bears, and these face extinction as their hunting grounds disappear. On the other hand there has been a worldwide increase in storms and consequential flooding, which also comes under her influence.

History of Global Warming and Retreating Ice in the Polar Regions

Around 12,000BC the Earth began thawing after the last Ice Age and the glaciers that had covered the northern hemisphere began retreating. It is estimated that there may have been a global population of around 4 million by 10,000BC, as opposed to over 6 *billion* now.[8] They were stone age hunter-gatherers who made jewellery, pottery, statues and hunting tools and we know that they enjoyed cave art, oil lamps and honey. But whilst the Ice Age was ending, there were some strange global phenomena, which the scientists of today puzzle about. The gradual and steady warming was inexplicably interrupted by sudden, extreme global cooling that spanned many years, a period called the Younger-Dryas.[9] At the University of Michigan they have been researching theories on just what could have happened 10,000 to 11,000 years ago to cause this sudden cold snap in the otherwise warming global climate. Apparently, during this time the Great Lakes were reduced to puddles. The universities eminent geologists are examining core samples to provide some evidence. This is essential to "help scientists predict the potential effects of rapid changes, produced by different factors, which are currently affecting Earth's climate," says the University of Michigan web site.[10] Their theory is that the amount of melt water didn't just raise sea levels, it threw the World's weather completely off balance.

Another eminent report from the National Academy of Sciences also discusses these extreme and rapid temperature shifts, but this one goes further by demonstrating not just the sudden drop in temperature, but also a huge leap of up to 16°C in the annual temperatures that followed it.[11]

The report said that these leaps could occur in the span of a mere decade. Confirmation of the information in that report came from another source, which stated that ice core records from Greenland showed a sudden warming of around 15°C in the annual mean temperature.[12]

All I can conclude is that Sedna was in the same part of her cycle that she is in now and there was an extreme global cooling and then warming.

Possibly connected to these weather events was another phenomena that occurred around this time period. Apparently at least 35 different species of large mammals were wiped out in North America. These included rhinos, woolly mammoths, the sabre-toothed cat, giant rabbits, horses and camels. In 2002, an anthropologist from the University of Washington in Seattle, a Dr Grayson,[13] said that he blamed global climate change or more specifically "rapid warming that triggered wide scale trauma". This guy was ahead of the game on climate change because he was blaming it long before the others in the field.[14] His peers were sticking to the theory that man had hunted and killed them into extinction.

Global Warming and Retreating Ice Now

In 2004, a few days before the announcement of Sedna's discovery, extremely eminent world-class climate scientists and academics issued frightening predictions of the effects of global warming via a leaked Pentagon defence advisor report:

"Climate change over the next 20 years could result in a global catastrophe costing millions of lives in wars and natural disasters….a former chief executive of the Meteorological Office likens the threat of climate change to that of terrorism…. the planet is carrying a higher population than it can sustain. By 2020 catastrophic shortages of water and energy will become increasingly harder to overcome, plunging the planet into war….the potential ramifications of rapid climate change would create global chaos."[15]

In March of 2006, the U.S. Environmental Protection Agency's own web site reported this:

> "new evidence that glaciers draining the ice sheets of Greenland and western Antarctica have recently accelerated – some of them more than doubling their speed over the past 5 years….rapid increase in glacial quakes during past 4 years. …simulations suggest that the climate in Greenland could become as warm by 2100 as it was …approx. 130,000 years ago. …an eventual sea level rise of as much as 20 feet in the coming centuries. …sea level rise could proceed at rates up to 3 feet per century."[16]

For the times they were written in, these were ground breaking. As strange as it may seem in later years, no one except un-published scientists and hippies left over from Greenham Common protests had heard of global warming before 2003. Reports like those above did start to emerge then, but they didn't really get a lot of media attention. By 2006 the whole subject was really taking off and newspapers started to devote pages and pages to the crisis. For instance, The Independent[17] gave it's whole front page to a photo of melting Polar ice and in a 6 page article inside, reported that there had been great and accelerated loss of usually permanent Artic ice. It had shrunk by 14% in just a few months between 2004 and 2005. That was compared to an average of 0.15% per year since records began in 1979. The melt rate had got 30 times faster in 1 year. The overall loss amounted to an area the size of Turkey and it had gone. Although Sedna had been discovered and there is no doubt that this was synchronous with the massive melt down, it didn't really become the top global issue until 2006. Likewise, in astrology, Sedna started to become really active in that year. The above report in the Independent appeared at such a time.

"The Inconvenient Truth" and The International Polar Year Initiative

At two crucial times for Sedna astrologically, there were some interesting events that made world news. In the first, around May 24th 2006, a film called The Inconvenient Truth starring Al Gore was released in the States. Until then, America, led by George Bush, was in denial about global warming. He had withdrawn America from Kyoto

Treaty that would have bound them to lowering CO_2 emissions. The next event was the launch of the International Polar Year Initiative, a large scientific programme focused on the Artic and Antarctic from March 2007.[18] This programme would be instrumental in getting world governments to pay attention to the crisis of melting ice. It found cataclysmic warming and loss of snowfall. The lack of snowfall is serious when you consider that usually, 100 billion snow crystals are manufactured by our planet every *second*.[19] This sort of production rate is necessary to maintain the climate in the icy regions. If it lessens, there are serious repercussions. However, if Sedna was giving less snow to the polar regions, she was certainly increasing precipitation elsewhere. If there is one thing the summers of 2007 and 2008 will be remembered for, it is rain….lots of it!

Sedna the Planet Could Be Used to Predict the Storms and Floods

From February 2006 until December 2008, Sedna the planet was in a relationship with another planet in the sky that made it easy to correlate weather events with her influence. As certain planetary formations occurred, there was a corresponding weather event here on Earth. In order to discount allegations that one can always find a storm or hurricane resulting in flooding somewhere on the planet, I used a certain rule to measure the validity of this coincidence. If the weather event was reported on Sky news in the news headlines, then it was big enough to be counted as extraordinary and linked with the specific astrological aspect of Sedna. Fortunately the specific astrological aspects are mathematical and precise so can be checked out by any astrologer. There were many correlations and I'll just give a brief summary of them:

"Inconvenient Truth" released May 2006
Global warming became hot news, September 2006
International Polar Year Initiative launched, March 2007
World Met Office[20] reported global land surface temperatures warmest ever and strongest rain ever, January-April 2007
Snow in South Africa, June 2007
Cyclone in Saudi Arabia, June 2007
Floods in North East England, June 2007

Floods in middle England, July 2007
Severe floods and death India, July 2007
Severe floods and death China, July 2007
Storm left over from Hurricane Joanna hits England, March 2008
American Mid West flooded, March 2008
Floods Ireland and Scotland, August 2008
Heavy rainfall England, September 2008

As I said before, these events had to severe enough to make the Sky news headlines on television. One observation I have made is that Sedna seems to be responsible for the rainfall and winds that cause the eventual flooding, rather than the flooding itself. The previous reports focus on the flooding because that has greater effect on our lives - people die, homes are lost and crops are ruined, but Sedna seems more responsible for the storms that caused the preceding immense quantity of rainfall.

The Tsunami of 2004 and the Sinking of Atlantis 12,000 Years Ago

The great storm summoned in her myth and her rulership over ocean life give us strong signposts to Sedna's meaning, so when the Indian Ocean suffered a massive tsunami in 2004, the year of Sedna's discovery, it was natural to associate the two things. It was certainly a very significant oceanic event, the biggest tsunami that the world has ever known with an estimated 200,000 killed.[21] According to the BBC, the Boxing Day sea surge was triggered when an earthquake caused the seabed to shoot up about 33 feet, moving the water above it. This turned into giant shock waves that travelled at speeds of up to 497 miles per hour. It may be too soon, however, to attribute this tsunami to Sedna alone and certainly there are astrological pointers that may implicate Makemake as being the god who resides over tsunamis.

However, there was a remarkable lack of loss of animal life that was commented on widely at the time. Elephants clearly knew it was coming and stampeded to high ground. Given Sedna's protection over the mammals of the deep, and animals in general, it would be in keeping with her spirit to save them. Many ancient cultures on Earth have a flood myth, from American Indians to the Babylonians to the

Irish to the Bible, so it is reasonable to assume that all these unrelated cultures actually do speak of some prehistoric huge flood that killed all but a few. But the Bible, at least, speaks of the careful saving of the animal species so they can re-populate and again, this is consistent with Sedna's theme.

On the other hand, the BBC[22] reported in 2005 that a Dr Gutscher had found sediment evidence of a large earthquake and tsunami that would have struck a submerged island in the Straits of Gibraltar around 12,000 years ago. This island, called Spartel Island, had once been above water and has been suggested as the likely candidate for the origin of the Atlantis legend. The Greek philosopher Plato wrote of Atlantis[23] and suggested that it sank in a huge one day event. He took his information from oral accounts that had been handed down over a period of 9,000 years and said this: "There occurred violent earthquakes and floods. And in a single day ... the island ... disappeared in the depths of the sea." He reported that Atlantis sat off the coast of North Western Africa and was inhabited by an advanced civilization. The interesting connection with Sedna is her cycle around the Sun of 10,500 years, in which she is nearest to the Sun for well over 500 years. Since that estimate may not be exact, or the 12,000 year time span for the sinking of Atlantis may differ by a few thousand years, it may make the 2 events synchronous. There is certainly enough evidence to at least include it in this chapter, whilst leaving the final answer to posterity.

Hurricane Katrina

This was also an extraordinary event, which happened in August 2005 and therefore, like the tsunami, it was before the 2006/08 period of high and consistent Sedna activity. But it was the most destructive hurricane ever to strike the United States and was almost certainly resonant with Sedna's energy. The planetoid was receiving energy from Mars, the planet of violent energy on this occasion, and he may have triggered this opening debut from her. However, Katrina had only been the third strongest hurricane in America's history. She was the deadliest because she hit the town of New Orleans, which is overcrowded and below sea level. When the flood barriers collapsed, the city flooded with 20 feet high water and that killed about 1,800 people.

This is a quote from a report issued by the United States Environmental Protection agency in 2006:

"The number of Category 4 and 5 hurricanes has increased by 80 per cent world wide during the past 35 years, according to a study in the 16/9/2005 issue of Science Magazine. Hurricanes in these two highest storm categories, with winds of 135 miles per hour or greater, now account for roughly 35% of all hurricanes, up from around 20% in the 1970's."[24]

They point out that the number of hurricanes hadn't grown, just the intensity. I'm including that as a counter argument to the possibility that Sedna's discovery has coincided with more extreme weather, maybe it was getting worse anyway and Sedna's effect just adds to a deteriorating situation. This same report has another interesting point. It specifically picks out Louisiana and South Florida and says that over the coming centuries they will "ultimately disappear under the rising seas." Since Hurricane Katrina had a big impact on Louisiana, should we not take it as a warning of the vulnerability of building and re-building cities on land that is already below sea level? Is it not a bit arrogant of Man to think that he can stop the rising water? This is not living within Mother Nature's limits; this is inviting her wrath and scorn. If Sedna was pointing this out with Hurricane Katrina and she has much more up her sleeve, it would be foolish not to be more respectful and obedient to what she foretells.

The Bird Flu Pandemic

I simply cannot ignore the synchronicities between the myth, Sedna's discovery and the bird flu pandemic that began in 2003, and became a world issue in 2004. After reading her myth, it is understandable that Sedna does not take too kindly to birds! However, it is more likely that pandemics in general come under the influence of Makemake since they are about population control and that is very much his issue.

Birds in general have great prominence in all the really ancient civilisations. One only has to look at the paintings on the walls of

Egyptian tombs to see that. It is interesting that birds were very important to civilisations as diverse as the North American Indians, the Polynesians, the Inuit tribes of Alaska and Greenland and the Egyptians. One of fascinations was their in-built migratory ability, which would help mark out the all-important dates in the agricultural calendar for certain tasks, such as planting. The birds use a whole spectrum of aids for navigation, including awareness of the position of the stars and the Earth's magnetic field. One, called the Artic Tern, actually follows the Sun[25] and flies from the Artic to the Antarctic, (from one end of the Earth to the other) thereby getting the maximum amount of sunlight possible on this planet! Because of the bird's great sensitivity to magnetic, solar and others rays in the electromagnetic spectrum, they are in dialogue with the spiritual energy of the 96% and unseen mysterious forces in general. You only have to listen to how they alert us to the impending sunrise with the dawn chorus to see that. The Ancients knew this and they worshipped them, for they understood that birds are naturally spiritual guides to the cycles of our Solar System. And that leads us very neatly to a passage about the Great Cycle.

The Great Cycles

As was said previously, planets closest to the Sun take about a year to make one complete circle around it. The new planets discovered in the Kuiper Belt, on the fringes of the Solar System, take two to three hundred years. Until now, that seemed like an enormous amount of time. Then we discover Sedna and now we are looking at 10,500 years to make one complete orbit of the Sun. This enormous time frame of 10,500 years obviously has great significance. We now have to accept that we are part of a *much* bigger cycle,[26] on a much bigger stage, in a much bigger play. Our horizons have really been pushed out. One of the effects of seeing a much bigger Universe, is to see ourselves as smaller and smaller grains of sand on a beach that just got 10,500 times bigger!

As we try and get our heads around that concept, then we can also take in to account some other big cycles that occur in our Solar System. Because of a wobble in the Earth's rotation we are in a cycle that is called the Great Cycle or Precession and takes 26,000(ish) years to complete. Planet Earth doesn't spin perfectly on its axis; it's like a spinning top that whizzes round and round very fast, but also has a slower wobble. A pencil sticking out of the top from the exact middle would draw a circle in the air above the top. This is what the Earth is doing. We don't notice it because it takes about 26,000 years for it to move round in the whole circle. Theoretically, if you sat in exactly the same place every year at the same time (ignoring leap years and summer times etc.) and looked through a tiny hole in a wall at a specific star in the sky, it should be in that same place every year of your life. That's because the Earth should have returned to exactly the same place each year. The star never moves, so it should all line up perfectly year after year. However, over the course of 72 years, it will appear to have moved ever so slightly. One degree to be precise. That's one degree out of the 360 that describe the dome of the sky all around you.

Anyway, as I said, the star hasn't moved, the Earth has. It may not be much, but over the course of hundreds or thousands of years the night sky changes dramatically because of this wobble. It means that the North Pole points in a different direction during the course of this 26,000 year movement. This in turn changes the direction and angle of the Sun's rays to the Earth and alters average temperatures and planetary conditions accordingly. Sedna is connected to climate change and particularly change at the polar region, where the land mass makes those areas more sensitive. This is because the land reacts more obviously to heating and cooling and the Sun can be full on or missing for months on end. Sedna's huge long oval cycle round the Sun puts her at different physical locations around the Sun in different millennia, and so she can accordingly describe different planetary climates. Cycles are funny things. There are really small ones, like the cycle of electrons whizzing round the nucleus of an atom and then there are bigger ones, like the Moon going around the Earth or the Earth going around the Sun. Then there are even bigger ones, such as the Earth's wobble, and then even bigger ones again. For instance our Sun is one of 100 million suns (stars) in our galaxy that spins around a centre and it takes about 225 million years for us to go around the centre once. This is called a galactic year.

By contemplating Sedna and her 10,500 year cycle around our Solar System we also contemplate our place and part in these mega cycles involving mega distances and mega time scales.

Evidence That We Have Done All This Before?

Amazingly, ancient civilisations knew of this wobble and it is possible that they tried to communicate this superior knowledge and other bits that we haven't worked out yet within the sacred geometry of their buildings. We just haven't worked out the messages yet. They knew their papyrus wasn't going to survive that long and only something as big and indestructible as the Pyramids could survive great floods, many thousands of years.......... and the Bush administration! It is a fallacy that pre-historic means lacking in sophistication and intelligence. They may have been far more advanced and developed than us in ways we don't understand yet.

For all we know, the human race is in a similar 11,000 year cycle to Sedna's. Physically, nothing remains of civilisations from before 5 – 6,000 years ago, anything existing before then has degraded into dust, so how can we prove otherwise? The scientists cannot agree on the accuracy of carbon dating old bones and they could be thousands of years out.

I read an interesting and puzzling report that made me wonder. In a journal called Nature,[27] two scientists from the Australian National University reported that around 10,000 years ago, fires caused changes in vegetation patterns and produced carbon dioxide emissions that apparently were the cause of global climate change. The pre-historic community "may have been actively engaged in modifying vegetation patterns, regional climate and atmospheric gas concentrations since long before the advent of modern concerns over global change. In short, the man-made activity that experts say is causing global warming now may actually be an ancient phenomenon" the scientists surmised.

Perhaps human civilisation is taken back to near extinction by a flood every 11,000 years, which wipes out all evidence of existing technology. Then we slowly grow to superiority as we have now, then devolve again as weather and planetary conditions deteriorate again. Like the movie Groundhog Day. Perhaps this is why we believe that civilisation emerged from places like Africa and the Middle East. Because they were least dependent on global support, such as electricity from Norway and water from Scotland. When the crunch came they could survive quite nicely on what they had always had. They lived on with water from their own well and crops from their own land. They won't perish when the seawater rises. The people living in major European cities are more dependent and vulnerable than our primitive cultures. In this way, when the water subsides and the planet has recovered, civilisation emerges from Iraq again!

What Can We Do?

On a Global Level

As Sedna represents Mother Nature or Sea-keeper of the oceans, then the message is that the `evil deeds` of humans are the terrible pollution and over-fishing that the seas have to bear. We are abusing the world`s oceans. Sedna is the symbol of a wake up call from Mother Nature. Each one of us must integrate into our conscious beings a sensitivity for our position as "caretaker of humanity and this planet"[28] or we face Sedna`s reminders! Lets look at planetary conditions in this latest Sedna awareness time. Is the current "wide scale trauma" now being caused by humans? If so, can we reverse it? According to the International Polar Year report, there is:

"......abundant evidence of changes in snow and ice: reductions in extent and mass of glaciers and ice sheets, reductions in area, timing, and duration of snow cover, and reductions in extent and thickness of sea ice.......Changes in the large ice sheets will impact global sea level, affecting coastal cities and low-lying areas. Changes in snowfall and shrinkage of glaciers will influence millions of people...... (the thaw) will mobilize vast reserves of frozen carbon, some of which, as methane, will increase the global greenhouse effect. Changes in sea ice combined with enhanced river inputs of freshwater will lead to substantial changes in ocean circulation. Warming of polar oceans, coupled with changes in ice coverage and river run-off, will alter marine ecosystems with consequences for globally-significant fisheries."[29]

Whether or not we caused it, we will have to live with it and make sensible decisions and plans for the future. Discussions might need to include a change to Christian beliefs that family planning is against the law of God. If the Christian God really wanted more than 6 billion living on this tiny planet why hasn't he prevented the above and ensured room for everyone? It's just a thought.

On a Spiritual Level

As I have just suggested, it may be time to return to pagan or spiritual beliefs that whole-hearted embrace the feminine energy of existence and re-awaken our conscious connection to the spiritual plane of existence. This includes connecting to our living, breathing planet; it's ethereal relationship to the Sun and the animals. We are not separate from them. For the last 2,000 years, Sedna's message has only been treasured by the esoteric minority and the deeply ethnic cultures, who in the main, do not run the planet. Sedna's sudden thrust into greater prominence symbolically, flags up her intention to be heard more clearly now.

Sedna's Inuit people have no organised religion and this may be further evidence that the Western world's invasive and restrictive religions may be out-moded or in decline. Strict attendance at purpose built mosques and churches for instance, may soon be a thing of the past. The Inuits were and are deeply spiritual, more so than the English, but they have never seen the need to have priests and formal religious structures around them.

I think we connect with Sedna when we seriously, properly and respectfully take care of the planet, the animals and the sea creatures, and accept Sedna's omnipresence in all things. She seems to say we have to get this right or pay dire consequences. We will have to accept and flow with the cycles we live in from the small one shown us by the Moon, to the large one of precession, but that does not spell our doom.

There are very strong fundamental reasons for the long-term success of the human race and I discuss those in the next chapter.

On a Personal Level

Those individuals with prominent Sedna energy will have experience of never really feeling completely at home in the sphere of personal relationships in some vague way. This might range from feeling a little awkward as though something is perhaps `missing` somehow, to some deep inner intangible fear of impending annihilation. The ability to feel completely safe might seem strangely elusive for some unknown reason.

It has been suggested[30] that people whose whole lives are influenced by Sedna's energy will demonstrate these themes. In the first part of their lives they may attract aggressive, angry and destructive people to them, then later they may comprehensively spurn and dismiss these types.

Sedna types might attract damaged lonely souls who themselves abuse and attack as a wounded animal will. Their lesson is to take no pooh, move out of this pattern, toughen up and get firm with this painful and damaging cycle. There are better, more fulfilling things lined up for them than this. They should embrace global issues, animals and the planet instead. Sedna types were born different and they hear a different drum beat. The lonely artic wastes of an un-fulfilling relationship will present them with no choice eventually. The howling gales will echo round their soul with the voices of a thousand screaming seagulls. They can shrivel up inside from the loneliness and cold around them, or you can spiritually surge into no-nonsense awareness of your own strength and authority. I'm not saying that one-to-one relationships are impossible for them, but they will struggle in the way that Sedna's struggled until they find a channel for all that cosmic and spiritual power. Then one-to-one relationships can be less stressed and laden with energies that shouldn't be played out in this area. Trying to extract or play out Sedna's powerful authority and familiarity with universal suffering in a relationship doesn't work. If you resonate to an energy that loves and feels for millions of lives, then how do you live this out within the limits of a little tiny personal relationship? You can't……the compassion is too immense, the victimisation needs to be too immense, the pain needs to be too immense.

Sedna feels at one with, and authority over, the whole of creation. As a planet she travels nearly to the next solar system and back. She feels the pain and loneliness of nearly 11,000 years on her own, and responsibility for the essence or soul of creation. If you have the capacity for that much awareness, it's hard to feel content just walking with hubby round Asda.

People who resonate with this should channel into animal charities. Become concerned about battery hens and birds, and all animals that are cruelly farmed and exploited. If you choose to eat animals, which Sedna is not opposed to in the myth, try to eat only those animals that you feel were properly respected.

Be more at peace with animals, and your awareness that everything is one and you are part of it. Feel your connectedness. Become a caretaker of the planet. The Pagans, Druids and Wiccans have understood this all along. Sedna has come to give this message a focus, and raise this awareness globally. The stakes are too high for any one of us to ignore it.

Chapter 10

" They fought from heaven; the stars in their courses fought against Sisera......"
The Book of Judges. 5:20

WHAT DOES THIS MEAN FOR US IN THE BUS QUEUE?

Looking back over these chapters, it is difficult to get a coherent sense of meaning. Where are we going with all of this? What`s going to happen this century? What`s going to happen to our children? Or even `In The End`?

The Doom Gloom Worst Case Scenario Bit

Let`s look at extreme worst-case scenarios. The very worst things that the arrival of all these new planets and the Kuiper belt could mean in astrology. Get a glass of wine first!

Well, last time Sedna was around, there was rapid climate change and many large species became extinct in extreme temperature fluctuations.

So that's one option. Makemake points out that the Easter Islanders initially lived in harmony with nature although they may have had a theorised large population. Then the Europeans arrived in the Pacific, causing de-population through a pandemic of infectious disease and kidnapping Islanders. Does this mean `foreigners` will arrive and wipe out most of us with diseases, or could it mean our ability to feed the world will diminish because we don't live in harmony with nature and the world is over-populated? That's another two options.

Option three concerns Ceres. Has she returned to guide us through the Underworld or walk with us in grief? Does her instruction to change the late 20th century attitude to death have a reason behind it? The Egyptian Initiates of the Mysteries used to achieve a comatose state and astral travel into higher spiritual awareness before returning to their bodies again. After this they celebrated the `other side' and feared death no more. Will we come to do the same? Then of course, there's Pluto-Charon. Does his message `survival of the fittest` and the regulation of souls on each plane of existence remind us that there are too many souls in bodies on our planet? Asclepios was flung to the stars as punishment for keeping too many souls alive; will our National Health Service be stopped too? (I'm not sure how much room they have up there in the stars for the whole of the N.H.S.) He also promotes the healing power of sex and unlimited, safe, clean nuclear power, so it can't be all bad.

And lastly, why have so many Earth Mother goddesses - Ceres, Sedna and Haumea all appeared at once? Possibly to reinforce seasonal cycles and the care and protection of nature and planet Earth. Think back for a moment, of how Ceres stopped the rain and dried out all the fields allowing us to bring the harvest home. But, of course, she is also responsible for grief plus appropriate death rites. Then there is Eris, a strong feminine energy and mighty and maverick defender; ready to stick her oar in with a very heavy hand to ruthlessly maintain universal Karma, Mana and Taboo.

But enough of this doom and gloom! I would now like to look at the insurances we have against these scenarios, plus what we have to believe in to reach for the silver lining, pot of gold, rainbow, cake and cherry. But before we do, I would like to just look at the prophesy of an ancient Greek philosopher.

The Gold, Silver and Iron Races

I am referring back, now, to the essay written by Hesiod, called Works and Days, which I examined in the Eris chapter. This document goes into precise and detailed instruction of how to use the rising and setting of various stars to carry out profitable management of farming and crops.

He urges us to avoid the anger of the deathless god/desses, which are wise words indeed, but it is his information of the 5 races that is most important[1].

First came a race of Gold – the golden age – and they lived in perpetual youth without care or toil. After death they became spiritual guardians and givers of wealth here on earth. The second race was silver and they suffered some woes because they were basically spoilt and molly-coddled their children. They had had it too good and they didn't see fit to worship the immortal gods. Since it is essential to honour the blessed god/desses, Zeus got fed up and put them way. Still, when they died, they did become immortal.

After the Silver things went even further down hill and along came the Bronze, who were strong and terrible. They had brutish, war-like ways and this time they had to suffer black death and go to Tartarus. The 4th race was before our own, nobler and righteous with many heroes who ranked as demi-gods. Their end was in a land of grain-giving earth and sweet flowing honey near an ocean at the ends of the Earth, but still they are untouched by sorrow.

Finally the fifth race, which Hesiod does not envy. This is the Iron race and they have to toil and work hard. Apparently some good men mingle with the evil ones and they die naturally when their hair turns grey. However, children dishonour their parents and chide them with bitter words. (Recognise anything yet?) It is at this point that envy, bad mouthing and scowling faces will make people wretched and no one will look after the elderly. (Any mother of teenagers will be leaning forward at this point.) Respect for justness and oaths will be lost and we will have earned our future, which is a fate of bitter sorrows with no help against evil.

So now we have that joyous prophesy under our belts, let's continue towards the pot of gold, rainbow, cake and cherry!

Reaching for Something Bigger or Shrinking to Smaller

Well, first of all, frontiers are expanding and our view of life has to widen along with our view of the Cosmos. We have to believe in and reach for something `bigger`. Or do we?

The Fears and Difficulties of Reaching for Bigger

Bigger has no meaning if we don't know what to use as a guide. What is bigger? Imagine that you have lived all your life in a small area. It wasn't uncomfortable and you were quite happy with it; but relative to the size of the planet it was infinitesimally small. You developed an understanding of this place and it was all you had to refer to when asked to imagine something else. You couldn't conceive of something bigger because you didn't know what `bigger` looked like. The only bigger you could come up with would be a bigger version of the little place you knew. So if your little place was in Egypt, then with all the desire in the world your concept of bigger would always be filled with sand and hot sun. You can't suddenly imagine snow and glaciers just because you are told to `think bigger`. Likewise, we can't just imagine what bigger is and be accurate.

So now we have a problem. We have to believe in something bigger and have faith in this, but there is absolutely no way that we are going to believe in something other than a bigger version of our little world. The best thing you can imagine if you have always lived in a desert is an oasis or a super-tent. Things that would help you deal with what you know. You wouldn't know how to dream of ice, not because you can't dream, but because your brain can't imagine ice without already having seen some. So we don't know what to dream of when we are told to think `bigger`.

Our second problem is our fear. We spend all our lives overcoming one fear after another. Fear of first going to school, fear of bogymen and the dark. Fear of loosing our parents, fear of not being able to earn enough money and fear of not finding the right relationship. Fear is our greatest motivator. The most potent teacher in our lives is fear. Most of our behaviour will ultimately be as a result of trying to avoid fear. It stands to reason then, that we are not going to be in a rush to take on more fear when we have quite enough for our lifetime, thank you very much.

On the surface of it, thinking of something bigger contains a lot of fear because it involves having to accept that we are not top of the pile and our lives are very small. And if this is the case then they are insignificant. And if they are insignificant then they could be at risk. Our attachment to them may be threatened and this invokes terrible fear that we might loose them. Then there is the usual fear of something we don't know or understand. It might harm us. If safety, survival and security are threatened then all the bigger concepts in the world are no substitute. No one with normal human emotions is going to happily substitute their home, children and career for belief in something `bigger`.

We do not want to see anything that we care about being put at risk for `bigger` until we can visualise, imagine or see it. Until we've understood it, read about it, tasted it and prodded it we are going to be fearful of it. Until a scientist has put it through rigorous double blind research studies and declared it `safe` it is not to be trusted and certainly no substitute for putting on the blinkers and keeping the small and narrow view. For most people believe that what they can't see can't harm them.

But what if bigger has been there all along? Not revealing itself, just keeping out of site and out of mind. Ok, we still can't conceptualise it but at this point we just have to accept it's there. This is the first stage in a process that will eventually lead to the lowering of fear. First, accept that bigger is there and in this century it will become known to us. As I said, like the Kuiper belt, it has been there all along. As you have got this far, we can definitely assume that you are willing to believe in something bigger, so what might this bigger be about?

So What Might `The Bigger Picture` be About?

The bigger picture is about accepting that we are just a tiny grain of sand on a beach that is exploding in size in the 21st century. But more than that, all the grains are linked into a giant invisible web. We could see this demonstrated very clearly in the first decade when the financial mistakes of one country suddenly showed themselves to be linked into the much bigger picture of world finances. Suddenly the un-payable loan that Mr Bloggs had taken out for his home in California was impacting on the car worker in the U.K. who now lost his job. Leaders of countries became very keen to point out that the financial circumstances of one country could not be isolated from another. Any other. A failing bank in Iceland caused big increases in local government taxes in some areas of the United Kingdom. This, of course, suited the leaders of countries who could now blame someone else for the gross mismanagement that had happened on their watch. Whatever. I'm really just using it as an example to demonstrate how things can all be linked into a much bigger picture without us even knowing.

So having accepted that we now have an inescapable bigger world to contend with lets look for the silver lining or pot of gold that will accompany this enlightenment. When looking at our place in a much bigger, spiritual, multiverse cosmos, we have to ask what is the spiritual and what is the meaning of life. What can we believe in that will give us the meaning for our existence and a heaven to work towards? Well just as the financial boundaries all dissolved and everything got linked up when we weren't looking, so should the world's spiritual beliefs. The previous boundaries and highly segregated religions that caused rivers of blood as men defended and aggressed to ensure the dominance of one religion over another serve no purpose. If we are all going to have the same bank soon, we may as well all have an accompanying flexible spiritual belief. This should go along the lines of Polynesian beliefs where all things are imbued with life force and divine energy and `death` is just the other side of the veil for a while. I hope you didn't miss that last sentence because it is one of the main points of this whole book. We need to adopt the eastern beliefs that divine life is an energy or force that is present in all things on this planet and we also need to understand that OUR life can exist in many other guises in many other planes of existence. This is what one aspect of bigger means.

Looking at Earthly Concerns and Possible Remedies

The population of Earth is becoming so big, it is unsustainable in it's current format, BUT, think back to the Egyptian desert example I used earlier in this chapter, where all we could imagine was a tent and an oasis when asked to dream up a solution. What if we cross the divide between what we can imagine (the super-tent and oasis) and get to the place where ice and snow are possibilities? Where there is ANY possibility. Ok, it won't be a format we recognise, and we may currently be tempted to dismiss it as science fiction `rubbish`, but maybe the day will come when we can travel somewhere other than Earth by whatever means. In any case, Makemake may make sure that the population will only be as big as its ability to grow sufficient local food. I never liked strawberries in December anyway.

National industrial growth at all costs may cease to be the holy grail of all governments. Otherwise there will be no governments. All global economic growth can achieve is the eventual consumption of all the natural resources of our planet. Nothing left to burn, nothing left to make things out of.

But……let's look even bigger and higher still. Let's look at the highest spiritual awareness the dwarf planets can give us and THERE we will find the answers we seek and the comfort we crave.

The Something We Have in the 4% That Absolutely Ensures Our Future

Before we are born, our soul agrees to be born again. And when we agree to this incarnation into life again, we do it joyously because there is something in the 4% that we can't have in the 96%. And that something is worth all the pain and hardship that we might have to bear now and anything that we might face in the future.

This `something` is an aspiration and achievement so great it means the whole of the Multiverse on all planes of existence will co-operate to keep our 4% going.

Something that we can't have on any other plane. Something that the spirits and angels long for. We know the god/desses long for it too, because we have so many myths telling us that they lived amongst mortal men. Why didn't they want to stay on Olympus or transcend into greater bliss and fusion with the Absolute Divine?

This `something` is ....(fan fare of trumpets).......

The desire for freedom and self-guidance.

Yep that's it! That bloody-minded, pig-headed need to express oneself as a single, autonomous individual, rather than part of the Divine One-ness in the highest reaches of Multiverse existence. For in the end, many spiritual layers up, there is no individuality at all, not even individual souls, just a will-less spiritual mass of refined energy and absolute perfection.

That said, we do still have some of the aspiration of the higher consciousness of the Multiverse, which seeks out fusion with this absolute spiritual perfection in the highest reaches of cosmic existence. This much we inherit from the divinity of the 96% and the higher Universal Mind; and looked at in its entirety, the whole journey generally seeks achievement through higher and finer grades of existence. But we do find it hard to let go of the self-gratification and self-direction that we enjoy in our Earthly incarnations, slopping around down here in the lower levels of existence.

Milton[2] describes this in his work `Paradise Lost` when the Fallen One says:

> "Here we may reign secure, and in my choice,
> To reign is worth ambition, though in hell!
> Better to reign in hell that serve in heaven…."

Helen Blavatsky[3] put it another way in 1888 when she wrote the Secret Doctrine. It says:

> "Better be man, the crown of terrestrial production and king over its opus operatum, than be lost among the will-less spiritual hosts in heaven."

Helen says that fall of man from spiritual being to earthly one is preferable. That he wants this hell on Earth because of

> "that law in nature, which implants in man as well as in every beast a passionate, inherent, and instinctive desire for freedom and self-guidance…"

For this reason; because all entities and divinities on all planes want to protect this single possible achievement so much; the 4% and this world will always be protected. It will never be allowed to become non-existent.

Human Worship is Needed to Feed the Spirit of the 96%

As I said in the Ceres chapter, the gods or spirits depend on our worship and feed off our emotions. Science tells us that dark particles called neutrinos pass through our body at the rate of millions per square centimetre per second. They pour out from our Sun and flood through the Earth 8 minutes later. We learnt in the chapter on Science that cell biologists have detected millions of signals passing through the ether in electromagnetic waves to the individual cells of our body where they are decoded by our nervous system and acted on. The neutrinos or signals carry with them our emotions. Our love and our passion and our grief. Which is why the love you generate can fill the Universe with its warmth. The god/desses or Spirit needs this to exist. And this is why the strongest of all the planets is currently Pluto-Charon. His message and sole (or soul) purpose is to regulate and maintain the existence of the 4% for all the Spirit in the Multiverse.

By the way, there is one other reason the god/desses want to maintain our plane of existence; which you may remember from the chapter on Ceres. This reason is found in the Egyptian Book of the Dead where one god moans to the Great Atum that in the existence beyond the Underworld there is "no drinking, breathing and lovemaking; **only** spirit being and contentment." The god/desses would rather have these earthly experiences than the bliss of fusion with the absolute perfection of the Universal mind. There is no way, therefore, that they will allow the demise of our world. I'll bet my last dollar on that.

World Religion and Religious Dynasties

So much wickedness has been perpetrated in the name of the religion in the last two thousand years, it is hard not to be scathing about it now. Catholic priests have repeatedly, determinedly and painfully raped young boys left in their care. Missionaries destroyed all the precious spiritual texts and festivals of the Easter Islanders, declaring their penis`s to be wicked. People who believed in astrology and herbalism were tortured for the sick pleasure of the deeply devout. Crusaders went to war to own and control a foreign land, murdering and eating the children of those who opposed them. And that's just Christianity. I don't even want to look at Islam and Judaism after that. And although it might be true to say that civilisation itself was relatively barbaric in those days; and all these things happened in context with the times, it is also true to say that some religious dynasties didn't demonstrate much compassion and tolerance. In fact compassion and tolerance have risen in stature and become more of an aspiration as the Christian church has *lost* it's authority and audience. This is an interesting possible correlation, but not one that either the church or the scientist will be in a rush to prove statistically. The church because the correlation might be right and the scientist because he's not interested!

Makemake and Haumea both symbolise change in religious beliefs. Our spirituality as a human race will move towards Eastern concepts such as Buddhism. Or perhaps the major religions will morph into something less controlling and structured. Something that dignifies animals and allows for many different god/desses. Something that will allow an individual response to spirituality and not demand it fits into the box and bows down to humanly controlled hierarchy.

But most of all it is going to have to give us the absolute conviction that peace, serenity and sublime fulfilment are achievable aspirations of the future. Whether that future is in a body or out of one. We want to know that as our loved ones and ourselves depart, we go to a comforting place that holds no fear. Come back pink and fluffy, all is forgiven. Remember, the Egyptian Initiates feared death no more. Isis/Ceres showed them higher spiritual consciousness and happiness. They learned that death was not final, that human souls are re-cycled and take on more life. That there is no death for life. Just as the seed is planted in the Underworld of the dark soil, so the soul goes into the Underworld to be born again. Jesus Christ wasn't the only one to experience resurrection. We all will.

Our religious framework of the future will have to give us this sort of reassurance and comfort. So that we don't fear death, we embrace the potential for moving on and know that we will return. Definitely and certainly. Then our religious and spiritual beliefs can support, calm and reassure us. Not fill us with the dread and fear of nothingness or divine retribution.

"The Key" From the Hermetic Texts, and the Key to it All

To get a good understanding of how our spirit, human body and mind are put together, it is illuminating to look at one of the writings from the Hermetic Texts. These writings are attributed to the mix of ancient Egyptian knowledge and Greek philosophical wisdom that emerged from 500B.C. through to 01A.D. They were probably the basis of the emerging religious dynasty and somehow survived the efforts to exterminate everything that preceded them. The texts are extraordinarily prophetic with very accurate descriptions of the 96%

and incredible spiritual insights. These insights are called gnosis, which means mysterious divine knowledge.

In The Key[4], there is a lovely description of how soul, spirit and mind are arranged within us. The human being is made up of layers that withdraw into the centre upon death; one at a time, from the outside in. Imagine 4 circles of decreasing size all sitting inside one another. The outer circle is the being's body. The next circle in is the spirit. The circle within this is the limit of the soul and this surrounds the smallest circle that represents the mind. In this way, the mind is in the soul, which is in the spirit, which is in the body. At death the spirit pulls inward from the outer body, pulling out of it's veins and heart and withdrawing into the soul and then the mind only. "And then the mind, stripped of wrappings and naturally divine takes unto itself a fiery body" and ascends. From there it assumes an energy state that it is too refined or rare for understanding. It is the thought or idea of the whole shebang and unknowable to us really. However, when mind, spirit and soul are together within us, mind will pull together with soul and spirit, becoming the motivation and energy of God that we can express and work with.

The Key gives a hierarchy of deity, putting a single almighty creator God at the top, with multiple and specific god/desses underneath and nature under that. Then comes human beings and they control "arts and science".
The trouble is we took control of "arts and science" and then took them too far. We introduced more and more gadgets, systems and complexity, which requires a great amount of planetary resources. But worse, we stopped believing in the god/desses. We thought we could just report straight to the top guy and the consequential monotheism took us into very misguided spiritual beliefs. We even have evidence of this in the Bible, which I point out in the chapter on Pluto. When this top God planted the Garden of Eden, why did he have something there that could, and did, spoil his idyll? He must have *had* to accept it. This tree represents the god/desses.

Unfortunately, the leaders of the world's three big religions took the single god at the top and ran with that at the expense of the multiple god/desses in the middle rankings. It doesn't work like that. You can't miss them out. You have to work with them or they will make themselves known as they are doing. There is no quick fix straight to the top, missing out the middle management. *For they are the 96%.* And although, as I said, they will protect humanity for it's enviable, independent self-governance, they will ultimately demand their share of the action too. If not, they will disrupt the whole shebang......... and then it will all have to start again.

We need to love our planets and their god/desses................then ....they will love us back!

REFERENCES FOR ALL CHAPTERS

CHAPTER 1 CHANGES ARE HAPPENING

[1] BLITZER, C. et al (1969) Great Ages of Man. A History of World`s Cultures. Age of Kings. International Edition, Amsterdam: Time Inc.

[2] O`CONNER, J.J. and ROBERTSON, E.F. (Sept 1996), Mathematical Discovery of Planets, School of Mathematics and Statistics, University of St. Andrews, http://www-history.mcs.st-andrews.ac.uk/Indexes/Astronomy.html [Accessed 27/7/2007]

[3] BLITZER, C. et al (1969) ibid.

[4] BOURNE, J.K. (2006) The Vaulting Pole. National Geographic, 210(6), pp.24

[5] BROWN, M. (13/7/2008), What`s In a Name (Part 2). Mike Brown`s Planets:http://www.mikebrownsplanets.com/2008/07/whats-in-name-part-2.html [accessed 6/10/2008]

[6] REANNEY, D. (1991) The Death of Forever. London: Souvenir Press Ltd.

CHAPTER 2 COOL SCIENCE

[1] CATHCART, B. (2005) The Fly in the Cathedral America: Farrar, Straus and Giroux

[2] DAVIES, P. and GRIBBIN, J. (1991) The Matter Myth. St. Ives, Great Britain: Viking

[3] LIPTON, B. Dr. (2005) The Biology of Belief. Llandeilo SA19 6YX UK: Cygnus Books.

[4] GEFTNER, A. (2008) Something From Nothing. NewScientist, Vol 199 (2674), pp.44.

[5] SHAPIRO et al. (2004) Revealing The Hidden Nature of Space And Time. Washington, D.C.: The National Academies Press.

[6] SAMPLE, I. (2008) The Idea of a Lifetime. NewScientist, 199 (2673), pp. 44-45.

[7] ANON. (27/9/2008) Nothing To LHC. New Scientist, 199(2675), pp6.

[8] ANON. L.H.C. The Large Hadron Collider. Various pages.
http://lhc.web.cern.ch/lhc/ [accessed 13/10/2008]

[9] XIAO-GANG, W (2006) Introduction to Quantum Many-boson Theory Articles and Lecture Notes: New States of Matter etc. Xiao-Gang Wen Home Site http://dao.mit.edu/~wen/pub/intr-frmb.pdf [Accessed 1/4/2007]

[10] WALTERS, R.J. (1997) The Language of the Cell Cell Science http://www.cellscience.com/chapter.htm]

[11] LIPTON, B. ibid.

CHAPTER 3 CERES, GODDESS OF GROWING AND GRIEVING

[1] WATANABE, S. (Jan 07 2002) A Texas Sized Space Rock NASA http://www.jpl.nasa.gov/news/features.cfm?feature=545 (06/09/2006)

[2] GEORGE, D., BLOCH, D., (2003) Asteroid Goddesses Berwick, Maine. Ibis press.

[3] SHIGA, D. (19th July 2008) Has Pluto sent us a message in Ceres?. New Scientist, 199 (2665), pp 10.

[4] SEYFFERT, O (1894) Dictionary of Classical Antiquities Ceres http://www.ancientlibrary.com/seyffert/pages/0129.gif (07/09/2006)

[5] NAGY, G., (5/11/2001) (Translation of) Homeric Hymn to Demeter, The University of Houston, http://uh.edu/~cldue/texts/demeter.html (12/8/2007)

[6] BOARDMAN, J., (1979) Athenian Red Figure Vases of the Archaic Period. London: Thames and Hudson.

[7] L. DA. COSTA Jr. W. Bro. Helio., (16/10/1999) The Chamber of Reflection. Grand Lodge of British Columbia.
http://freemasonry.bcy.ca/texts/gmd1999/pondering.html

[8] WATTERSON, B., (1999) Gods of Ancient Egypt. Stroud: Sutton Publishing Ltd.

[9] BRUNTON, P., (1988) A Search in Secret Egypt. York Beach, Maine: Samuel Weiser, Inc.

[10] FAULKNER, R. et al (1998) The Egyptian Book of the Dead. San Francisco: Chronicle Books LLC

[11] SEYFFERT, O. (1984) ibid.

[12] SAMPLE, I., (31/8/2007), Global food crisis looms as climate change and population growth strip fertile land. The Guardian. http://www.guardian.co.uk/environment/2007/aug/31/climatechange.food [20/7/2008]

[13] BOARDMAN, J., (1980) Athenian Black Figure Vases. London: Thames and Hudson.

[14] NILSSON, M. (1940), Greek Popular Religion. Sacred Texts. http://www.sacred-texts.com/cla/gpr/gpr07.htm [12/08/2007]

CHAPTER 4 PLUTO, LORD OF THE INVISIBLE REALMS

[1] BULFINCH, T. (1978) Bulfinch`s Mythology. U.S.A. Avenel.

[2] ANON. (1971) The Living Bible. Sussex: Tynedale House Publishers.

[3] HAND, R. (1976) Planets in Transit: life Cycles for Living. U.S.A.: Whitford Press.

[4] BLAVATSKY, H.P. (1888) The Secret Doctrine: The Synthesis of Science, Religion and Philosophy. Sacred Texts. http://www.sacred-texts.com/the/sd/sd1-0-co.htm#preface [Vol1pp459footnotes] [accessed10/8/2008]

[5] DANIELOU, A. (1991) The Myths and Gods of India. Vermont: Inner Traditions Int. Ltd.

[6] DANIELOU, A. ibid. pp198

[7] WATTERSON, B. (1999) Gods of Ancient Egypt. Stroud: Sutton Publishing Ltd. pp67

[8] WATTERSON, B. ibid. pp68

[9] WEST, J.A. (1993) Serpent in the Sky, The High Wisdom of Ancient Egypt. 2nd ed., Illinois: Quest Books

[10] WATTERSON, B. ibid.

[11] VAN DEN DUNGEN, W, (2001) On the Shabaka Stone. Sophiatopia. http://www.maat.sofiatopia.org/shabaka.htm [accessed 14/8/2008}

[12] CATHCART, B. (2005) The Fly in the Cathedral America: Farrar, Straus and Giroux

[13] GOODMAN, L. (1987) Linda Goodman`s Star Signs. (2nd ed.) London: Pan Books Ltd.

[14] LEO, A. (1983) Esoteric Astrology. (2nd ed.) Vermont: Destiny Books Ltd.

[15] GREENE, L. (1976) SATURN, A New Look at an Old Devil Maine, U.S.A. Samuel Weiser, Inc.

[16] WEST, J.A. ibid. pp64

[17] ALEXANDER, A. (22nd June 2006) Nix and Hydra Join Pluto`s Family The Planetary Society. http://www.planetary.org/news/2006/0622_Nix_and_Hydra_join_Plutos_Family.html [accessed 5/11/2006]

[18] ALEXANDER, A. (3rd November 2005) Hubble Observations Add Two New Moons to Pluto The planetary Society. http://www.planetary.org/news/2005/1103_Hubble_Oberservations_Add_Two_New_Moons:html [accessed 5/11/2006]

[19] BLAVATSKY, H. P. (1888) The Secret Doctrine: The Synthesis of Science, Religion and Philosophy Sacred Texts:(Vol. 2, pp 488) http://www.sacred-texts.com/the/sd/sd2-2-04.htm [accessed 19/9/2008]

[20] GOODMAN, L. ibid.

[21] BOOTH, E.R, Dr. (1906) History of Osteopathy Meridian Institute www.meridianinstitute.com/eant/files/booth/chapter10.htm [accessed 9/11/2006]

[22] BLANEY, Dr K., (2002) The Caduceus Versus the Staff of Asclepius. Dr Keith T Blaney: http://drblayney.com/Asclepius.html [accessed 15/11/2006]

[23] FICINO, A. (2001)Late Antiquity: Hermetica. Ralph Abraham, PhD http://www.ralph-abraham.org/ficino/newbook/ch2.pdf (pp19) [accessed 14/11/2006]

[24] TEGMARK, M. Multiverse Massachusetts Institute of Technology http://www.space.mit.edu/home/tegmark/multiverse1.html [accessed 8/8/08]

[25] BARTLETT, D. et al, (2003) The Elegant Universe, Welcome to the Eleventh Dimension. NOVA: http://www.pbs.org/wgbh/nova/transcripts/3014_elegant.html [accessed 17/2/2009]

[26] NOELS, C. 14/1/1999 The History of the L.H.C. Project. LHC The Large Hadron Collider: http://lhc.web.cern.ch/lhc/general/history.htm [accessed 16/9/2008]

[27] ELBARADEI, M. Dr. (27/6/2004) Nuclear Power: A Look At The Future. I.A.E.A.: http://www.iaea.org/NewsCenter/Statements/2004/ebsp2004n005.html [accessed on 17/9/2008]

[28] DANIELOU, A. ibid. (pp217)

[29] BLANEY, Dr K., (2002) The Caduceus Versus the Staff of Asclepius. Dr Keith T Blaney: http://drblayney.com/Asclepius.html

[30] BROOKS, M. (2008) The Power of Belief. New Scientist. 199(2670) pp26-39

CHAPTER 5 CHARON, OUR GUIDE TO PLUTO AND THE INVISIBLE REALMS

[1] ANON. (20/6/2003) 25th Anniversary of the Discovery of Pluto`s Moon, Charon. U.S. Naval Observatory: http://www.usno.navy.mil/pao/press/charon.shtml [accessed 3/9/2008]

[2] ARNETT, B. (21/4/2008) Charon. The Nine Planets: http://www.nineplanets.org/pluto.html#charon [accessed 3/9/2008]

[3] ANON. (August 2006) Planet Definition Question and Answer Sheet; International Astronomical Union: http://www.iau.org/public_press/news/release/iau0601/q_answers/ [accessed 4/9/2008 and 18/2/2009]

[4] BULFINCH, T. (1978) Bulfinch`s Mythology. U.S.A. Avenel.

[5] CAMPION, N. (2008) The Dawn of Astrology. London. Continuum Books

[6] BULFINCH, T. ibid.

[7] RADICE, B. (1973) Who`s Who in the Ancient World. 2nd ed., Middlesex: Penguin Books

[8] RADICE, B. ibid.

[9] COTTERELL, A. (2000) World Mythology. Parragon: London.

[10] ATSMA, A. Nyx. THEOI Greek Mythology: http://www.theoi.com/Protogenos/Nyx.html [accessed 30/9/2008]

[11] MERCER, S (1952) Texts of Miscellaneous Contents; The Pyramid Texts: http://www.sacred-texts.com/egy/pyt/pyt49.htm

[12] PRITCHARD, J. (1955) Ancient Near Eastern Texts Relating to the Old Testament. 2nd Ed. New Jersey: Princeton. (pp91)

[13] REANNY, D. (1995) The Death of Forever. 2nd ed., London: Souvenir Press.

[14] LINDSTROM, M. et al. (13/6/2008) Pluto. N.A.S.A. http://solarsystem.jpl.nasa.gov/planets/profile.cfm?Object=Pluto&Display=Overview

CHAPTER 6 MAKEMAKE, GREAT SEA SPIRIT OF EASTER ISLAND

[1] BROWN, M. (2008) What`s In a Name? Part 2. Mike Brown`s Planets: http://www.mikebrownsplanets.com/2008/07/whats-in-name-part-2.html [accessed 07/10/2008]

[2] FLENLEY, J. and BAHN, P. (2002) The Enigma of Easter Island. New York: Oxford University Press. [pp 13]

[3] HEYERDAHL, T. (1958) Aku-Aku The Secret of Easter Island. 2nd ed., London: Tinling and Co. [pp.317]

[4] SMART, N. (1989) The World`s Religions. 2nd ed., Cambridge. Cambridge University Press.

[5] RUGGLES, C. (2005) Ancient Astronomy. California; ABC-CLIO.

[6] FINNEY, B. (2005) Applied Ethnoastronomy: Navigating By The Stars Across The Pacific. in CHAMBERLAIN et al. (ed) Songs From The Sky. United Kingdom: Oscarina Books, [pp336.]

[7] LOW, S. Gift of the Wind, Aboard Hokule`a on Her Miraculous Journey to Rapa Nui. Polynesian Voyaging Society. http://pvs.kcc.hawaii.edu/rapanui/samleg3.html (accessed 23/10/2008)

[8] FLENLEY and BARN ibid. pp75.

[9] FLENLEY and BARN ibid. pp42.

[10] ANON., The Statues of Easter Island. Extracts From Lectures by Thor Heyerdahl Bradshaw Foundation: http://www.bradshawfoundation.com/thor/index.php [accessed 14/11/2008]

[11] HEYERDAHL, T. ibid.

[12] HOLMES, B. (2006) Did Humans Devastate Easter Island on Arrival? New Scientist: http://www.newscientist.com/article.ns?id+dn8825&print=true

[13] THOMPSON, W. (1891) Te Pito Te Henua, Or Easter Island. Sacred Texts: http://www.sacred-texts.com/pac/ei/ei00.htm [pp463]

[14] FISCHER, S. (2005) Island At The End of The World. London: Reaktion Books Ltd. pp50.

[15] FISCHER, S. ibid. pp74

[16] YOUNG, E. (31/7/2006) Easter Island: A Monumental Collapse? NewScientist.com: http://www.newscientist.com/article.ns?id=mg19125621.100&print=true (accessed 23/10/2008)

[17] FISCHER, S. ibid. pp 89.

[18] FISCHER, S. ibid. pp 99.

[19] FLENLEY and BARN. ibid.

[20] THOMPSON, W. ibid. pp 473.

[21] THOMPSON, W. ibid. pp 463.

[22] THOMPSON, W. ibid. pp 459.

[23] ENGLERT, S. (1972) Island At The Centre of The World. London: Robert Hale and Co. [pp65]

[24] CARROLL, A. (1892) The Easter Island Inscriptions And The Translation And Interpretation Of Them. Journal of the Polynesian Society. http://www.rongorongo.org/carroll/105.html

[25] THOMPSON, W. ibid. pp 535.

[26] RJABCHIKOV, S. (1998) Several Rongorongo Records. Symbolism of Archaic Beliefs. Anthroglobe. http://www.anthroglobe.info/docs/Sergei/Rongorongo-records.htm [accessed 24/7/2008]

[27] FISCHER, S. ibid. pp76.

[28] THOMPSON, W. ibid. pp471

[29] FISCHER, S. ibid. pp73.

[30] RUGGLES, C. ibid. pp140

[31] RUGGLES, C. ibid. pp407.

[32] VAN TILBERG, J. (2000) Secrets of Easter Island, Stone Giants: NOVA Online: http://www.pbs.org/wgbh/nova/easter/civilization/giants.html

[33] THOMPSON, W. ibid. pp499.

[34] HUNT, T. and LIPO, C. (2005) Mapping Prehistoric Statue Roads on Easter Island http://www.anthropology.hawaii.edu/projects/rapanui/lipo&hunt%202005.pdf [accessed 23/11/2008]

[35] THOMPSON, W. ibid. pp498.

[36] CARROLL, A. (1892) The Easter Island Inscriptions And The Translation And Interpretation Of Them. Journal of the Polynesian Society. http://www.rongorongo.org/carroll/105.html [accessed 24/7/2008]

[37] ENGLERT, S. (1980) Histories, Legends and Traditions of Easter Island. The Rongorongo of Easter Island: http://www.rongorongo.org/leyendas/034.htm [28/10/2008]

[38] ANON. Earthquake of Peru; USGS: http://earthquake.usgs.gov/regional/world/peru/history.php [accessed 3/12/2008]

[39] THOMPSON, W. ibid. pp499.

[40] FLENLEY and BAHN. Ibid. pp15.

[41] HOLMES, B. Beastly Tales. New Scientist. 197(2639), pp.30-33.

[42] TILBURG, J. (1994) Easter Island, Archaeology, Ecology and Culture U.S.A.: Smithsonian Institution Press

[43] ORLOVE, S. et al (2000) Forecasting Andean rainfall and crop yield from the influence of El Nino on Pleiades visibility. Nature, 403, pp68-71. (Kindly sent to me by Bill Law, President of the Walsall Astronomy Group.)

[44] DE SANTILLANA, G. and VON DECHEND, H. (1969) Hamlet`s Mill. An Essay Investigating the Origins of Human Knowledge and its Transmission Through Myth. New Hampshire. Godine Publisher Inc. [pp164]

[45] ALLEN, M. (15/5/2007) Three Millennia of Human and Sea Turtle Interactions In Remote Oceania. Sea Turtle Organisation: http://74.125.77.132/search?q=cache:xUky09BYpFQJ:www.seaturtle.org/PDF/Allen_

2007_CoralReefs.pdf+turtles,+polynesia.+migratory+pattern,+breeding,+arrival&hl=en&ct=clnk&cd=1&gl=uk [accessed 24/12/2008 – seriously!]

46 YOUNG, E. (12/4/2008) Ocean Biodiversity: Depths of Ignorance. NewScientist: http://www.newscientist.com/article/mg19826511.700-ocean-biodiversity-depths-of-ignorance.html [accessed 25/12/2008 - seriously!]

47 PEARSON, A. (2009) Perfect Storm. NewScientist. 201(2689), pp. 32-35

48 DE SANTILANA, G. and VON DECHEND, H. (1969) Hamlet`s Mill. An Essay Investigating The Origins Of Human Knowledge And It`s Transmission Through Myth. New Hampshire: David R Godine Inc.

49 DE SANTILANA, G. and VON DECHUND, H. (1969) ibid.

50 BILLIMORIA, N. The Panis of the Rig Veda and Script of Mohenjo Daro and Easter Island. Journal of the Polynesian Society. Vol 48. http://www.rongorongo.org/theories/indus/bill092.html pp93 [accessed 26/10/2008]

51 BILLIMORIA, N. ibid. pp96

52 FISCHER, S. ibid. p57

53 YOUNG, E. (31/7/2006) Easter Island: A Monumental Collapse? NewScientist.com: http://www.newscientist.com/article.ns?id=mg19125621.100&print=true [accessed 23/10/2008]

54 THOMPSON, W. ibid. pp490.

55 ENGLERT, S. ibid.

CHAPTER 7 GODDESS OF HAWAII, BIRTH, NATURE, ROCK AND FIRE

1 COURTLAND, R. (19/9/2008), Controversial Dwarf Planet Finally Named Haumea; New Scientist: http://www.newscientist.com/article/dn14759-controversial-dwarf-planet-finally-named-haumea.html

2 McKEE, M. (29/7/2005), New World Found in Outer Solar System; New Scientist: http://www.newscientist.com/article/dn7751-new-world-found-in-outer-solar-system.html

[3] BROWN, M. (2006) Haumea; California Institute of Technology, http://www.gps.caltech.edu/~mbrown/2003EL61/

[4] SCHILLING, G. (15/10/2008) Dwarf Planet`s Body Parts Litter the Solar System; New Scientist: http://www.newscientist.com/article/dn14954

[5] BECKWORTH, M. (1940) Hawaiian Mythology; Sacred Texts: http://www.sacred-texts.com/pac/hm/hm21.htm (accessed 31/1/2009)

[6] LILIUOKALANI, Queen of Hawaii, (1897) An Account of the Creation of the World According to Hawaiian Tradition. Sacred Texts: http://www.sacred-texts.com/pac/lku/lku01.htm (accessed 3/2/2008)

[7] BECKWORTH, M. ibid. pp 304

[8] BECKWORTH, M. Ibid. pp 279

[9] RUGGLES, C. Ancient Astronomy. Santa Barbara U.S.A.: ABC-CLIO pp178.

[10] LILIUOKALANI, ibid

[11] RALOFF, J. (23/1/2009), Darkness, Melatonin May Stall Breast and Prostate Cancers: ScienceNews: http://www.sciencenews.org/view/generic/id/40170/title/Darkness,_melatonin_may_stall_breast_and_prostate_cancers_ [accessed 3/2/2009]

[12] BECKWORTH, M. Ibid. pp 306

[13] MALY, K. (2001) An Overview of The Hawaiian Cultural Landscape. Kumupono. http://kumupono.com/Hawaiian%20Cultural%Landscape.pdf.

CHAPTER 8 ERIS, GODDESS OF STRIFE, STIMULATION AND RIVALRY

[1] LAKDAWALLA, E. (30/7/2005) The Planetary Society Weblog. http://www.planetary.org/blog/article/00000176/ [accessed 27/8/2006]

[2] Taken from leaflet issued with a video. Xena Warrior Princess Video 1996 Universal Television Enterprises, Inc. as assigned to Studio USA Television Distribution LLC. Universal Pictures (UK) Ltd.

[3] TINDOL, R. (2006) The Dwarf Planet Formerly Known As Xena Has Officially Been Named Eris, I.A.U. Announces; Caltech Media Relations: http://pr.caltech.edu/media/Press_Releases?PR12893.html

[4] TINDOL, R. ibid.

[5] SEYFFERT, O. (1894), Dictionary of Classical Antiquities. Ancient Library. http://www.ancientlibrary.com/seyffert/0228.html [accessed 2/3/2009]

[6] SEYFFERT. O. ibid.

[7] SEYFFERT, O. ibid. pp225

[8] HAYS, M.H. (1918) Notes on the Works And Days of Hesiod. Ph.D. Dissertation, Faculty of the Graduate School of Arts and Literature, University of Chicago. http://www.archive.org/stream/notesonworksdays00haysrich /notesonworksdays00haysrich_djvu.txt [accessed 21/2/2009]

[9] HAYS, M.H. ibid.

[10] BULFINCH, T. (1978) Bulfinch`s Mythology. U.S.A. Avenel

CHAPTER 9 SEDNA, THE PRIDE AND OUTRGE OF THE GREAT OCEAN GODDESS

[1] BROWN, M. (2004) Sedna. Caltech http://www.gps.caltech.edu/%7Embrown/sedna/ (accessed 27/08/2006)

[2] BROWN, M. Sedna. Ibid.

[3] BROWN, M. Sedna. Ibid.

[4] BOAS, F. (1888) Sedna and the Fulmar. in FOWKE, E. (ed) Folklore of Canada. Ontario, Canada: The Canadian Publishers, pp 41-42

[5] HEFNER, A. (2002-2007) Sedna. Mythical Folk. http://www.themystica.org/mythical-folk/~articles/s/sedna.html

[6] HEFNER, A. (2002-2007) Adlivun Mythical Folk. http://www.themystica.org/mythical-folk/~articles/a/adlivun.html

[7] KENTON, M. (2005, July 26) The Animal and the Human. *EzineArticles.* http://www.ezinearticles.com/?The-Animal-and-the-Human&id=54222 (accessed 30/8/06)

[8] ROHDE, D. (11/11/2003) On the Common Ancestors of All Living Humans; Massachusetts Institute of Technology: http//citeseerx.ist.psu.edu

[9] PIDWIRNY, M. (Lead Author); Maggie L. Walser (Topic Editor). 2007. "Earth's climatic history." In: Encyclopedia of Earth. Eds. Cutler J. Cleveland (Washington, D.C.: Environmental Information Coalition, National Council for Science and the Environment). [Published in the Encyclopedia of Earth December 31, 2007; Retrieved May 9, 2009]. http://www.eoearth.org/article/Earth's_climatic_history

[10] POBOJEWSKI, S., (Oct 26 1992) Changes in lakes levels 10,000 years ago could explain global chill. News and Information Services. http://www.umich.edu/~urecod/9293/Oct26_92/22.htm (accessed 4/9/2006)

[11] National Academy of Sciences. (2006) Abrupt Climate Change: Inevitable Surprises. National Academy of Sciences. http://dels.nas.edu/abr_clim/evidence.shtml (accessed 2/9/2006)

[12] ANON (29/7/2003) Abrupt Climate Change;National Geophysical Data Center. http://www.ngdc.noaa.gov/paleo/ctl/abrupt.html (accessed 4/9/2006)

[13] MOULTON HOWE, L. (2002) What Happened That Killed So Many Animals? Cambodia News online. http://www.cambodianonline.net/earth02002.htm (accessed 27/8/2006)

[14] SCHWARTZ, J. (24/10/2001) Blame North American Megafauna Extinction on Climate Change, Not Human Ancestors. University of Washington. http://www.washington.edu/newsroom/news/2001archive/10-01archive/k102401.html (accessed 10/5/2009)

[15] TOWNSEND, M., and HARRIS, P., (Feb 22nd 2004) Now the Pentagon tells Bush: climate change will destroy us Guardian Unlimited http;//www.guardian.co.uk/usa/story/0,12271,1153531,00 .html (accessed 31/8/2006)

[16] U. S. Environmental Protection Agency. (2006) Global Warming News and Events, Science and Policy News. U.S. Environmental Protection Agency. http:Yosemite.epa.gov/oar/global warming.nsf/content/News and eventsScience and Policy News.html (accessed 31/8/2006)

[17] McCARTHY, M. and USBORNE, D. (15/9/2006) Massive Surge In Disappearance of Arctic Sea Ice Sparks Global Warming. The Independent. No 6212. pp1-5

[18] ANON. (March 2007) About IPY: International Polar Year: http://www.ipy.org/index.php?/ipy/about/ (accessed 3rd May 2009)

[19] ANON, (9/5/2009) Polar Bear Week With Nigel Marvin. Channel Five Broadcasting Corporation. (watched 9/5/2009)

[20] RICHARD-VAN MAELE, C. (7/8/2007) The World Meteorological Organization Reports on Extreme Weather and Climate Events. World Meteorological Office. http://www.wmo.int/pages/mediacentre/press_releasespr_791_en.html (accessed 3/5/2009)

[21] ANON. (2008) 2004: Thousands Die in Asian Tsunami. BBC. http://news.bbc.co.uk/onthisday/hi/dates/stories/december/26/newsid_4631000/4631713.stm (accessed 5/5/2008)

[22] ANON, (15/8/2005) Tsunami Clue to Atlantis Found BBC News. http://news.bbc.co.uk/1/hi/sci/tech/4153008.stm (accessed 31/8/2006)

[23] ORNELAS, G. Atlantis Rises Again. Science Magazine; http://sciencenow.sciencemag.org/cgi/content/full/2005/722/1 (accessed 10/5/2009)

[24] ANON. (2006) Science and Policy News. U.S. Environmental Protection Agency. http://yosemite.epa.gov/oar/globalwarming.nsf/content/NewsandeventsScienceandPolicynews.html (accessed 31/8/2006)

[25] MEAD, C. (1983) Bird Migration. Middlesex. Country Life Books.

[26] BROWN, R., (May 2005) Sedna Astrological Meaning: evolving thoughts. Karma Astrology. http://www.karmastrology.com/Sedna-meaning.shtml (accessed 27/08/2006)

[27] ANON, (19/8/1998) Rise In fires Began 10,000 Years Ago. Forests.Org: http://forests.org/archive/general/risefire.htm (accessed 27/8/2006)

[28] BROWN, R., (May 2005) Sedna Astrological Meaning: evolving thoughts Karma Astrology. http://www.karmastrology.com/Sedna-meaning.shtml (accessed 27/08/2006)

[29] ANON, (March 2007) About IPY; International Polar Year: http://www.ipy.org/index.php?/ipy/about/ (accessed May 3rd 2009)

[30] BROWN, R. (May 2005) Sedna Astrological Meaning Evolving Thoughts. Karma Astrology. http://www.karmastrology.com/Sedna-meaning.shtml

CHAPTER 10 WHAT DOES THIS MEAN FOR US IN THE BUS QUEUE?

[1] HAYS, M.H. (1918) Notes on the Works And Days of Hesiod. Ph.D. Dissertation, Faculty of the Graduate School of Arts and Literature, University of Chicago. http://www.archive.org/stream/notesonworksdays00haysrich/notesonworksdays00haysrich_djvu.txt [accessed 21/2/2009]

[2] MILTON, J. (1667) Paradise Lost: New Arts Library: http://www.paradiselost.org/novel.html [accessed 3/3/2009]

[3] BLAVATSKY, H. (1888) The Secret Doctrine: sacredtexts.com: http://www.sacred-texts.com/the/sd/index.htm

[4] MEAD, G.R.S. (1906) Thrice Great Hermes Vol 2: Sacred Texts: http://www.sacred-texts.com/gno/th2/index.htm

ILLUSTRATIONS

Illustration 1 - Pre 17th century Solar System. Designed by Alison. Drawn by Robbi Lambert.

Illustration 2 - 19th century Solar System. Designed by Alison. Drawn by Robbi Lambert.

Illustration 3 - 21st century Solar System. Designed by Alison. Drawn by Robbi Lambert

Illustration 4 – Ceres. Designed by Alison. Drawn by Robbi Lambert

Illustration 5 – The Greek Underworld. Copied from Athenian Black Figure Vases by John Boardman. He describes it as a neck amphora by the Bucci painter. Souls pour water and Sisyphos rolls his stone in Hades. Drawn by Robbi Lambert.

Illustration 6 – Pluto, Proserpine, Mercury and a mortal. Copied and adapted from The Encyclopaedia of Mythology(1996) by Authur Cotterall, which reports it to have been copied from an earlier illustration in Dr. Smith`s Classical Dictionary, 1895. Drawn by Robbi Lambert

Illustration 7 – Charon, Hermes and a mortal. Copied from an image on www.theoldreligion.com, source not supplied. Drawn by Robbi Lambert.

Illustration 8 – Mekemeke, the Great Sea Spirit. Copied from a drawingin W illiam Thompson's report. This rare image was drawn by Thompson from a rock carving. The report can be seen on www.sacred-texts.com Drawn by Robbi Lambert.

Illustration 9 - Adapted from Island At The End of The World by S. Fischer. Drawn by Robbi Lambert.

Illustration 10 – Copy of a drawing done by a member of Captain Cooke's party in 1774. Copied by Robbi Lambert.

Illustration 11 - Photocopy from The Easter Island Tablets: Decipherments, by A Carroll, published in the Journal of the Polynesian Society, Vol 1 (1892)
This is all on the rongorongo web site at www.rongorongo.org/carroll/tahua.html

Illustration 12 and 13 – Drawn by Robbi Lambert from the many different images available in the books in the reference section.

Illustration 14 - Drawn by Robbi Lambert from the many different images available in the books in the reference section.

Illustration 15 – Drawn by Robbi Lambert from an illustration by William Thompson in his report entitled Te Pito Te Henua Or Easter Island. www.sacred-texts.com/pac/ei/index.htm

Illustration 16 - Drawn by Robbi Lambert from the many different images available in the books in the reference section.

Illustration 17 – Hawaii. Drawn by Robbi Lambert

Illustration 18 – Eris. Drawn by Robbi Lambert

Illustration 19 – Sedna. Drawn by Robbi Lambert

Image on the front cover: credit Greg Bacon (STScI/AVL) and the Hubble Telescope project at
http://hubblesite.org/newscenter/archive/releases/2001/38/image/a/
This is an artists impression of a Jupiter-like giant gas planet orbiting a yellow Sun.

Image on the back cover: credit Jimmy Westlake, Colorado Mountain College at http://apod.nasa.gov/apod/ap070525.html
This real photograph shows the Milky Way, Jupiter and Vesta, the asteroid.
My thanks to Prof. Westlake for allowing me to use the stunning photo.